Old Houses, New Houses

Old Houses, New Houses

... And 30 Other Bible-Based Meditations

Series # 11

Roger and Sylvia Ellsworth

Unless otherwise noted, Scripture quotations are taken from the New King James Version®. Copyright © 1982 by Thomas Nelson. Used by permission. All rights reserved.

Copyright © 2018, Roger Ellsworth

All rights reserved. No part of this book may be reproduced, scanned, or distributed in any printed or electronic form without permission.

First Edition: 2018

ISBN: 978-0-9600203-1-7

20181115LS

Great Writing Publications
www.greatwriting.org
Taylors, SC

www.greatwriting.org

Purpose

My Coffee Cup Meditations are short, easy-to-read, engagingly presented devotions based on the Bible, the Word of God. Each reading takes a single idea or theme and develops it in a thought-provoking way so that you are inspired to consider the greatness of God, the relevance of the good news of the life, death, resurrection, and coming-again of Jesus, and are better equipped for life in this world and well prepared for the world to come.

www.mycoffeecupmeditations.com

https://www.facebook.com/MyCoffeeCupMeditations/

Dedication

Dedicated to the Memory of:

William Hendriksen

Martyn Lloyd-Jones

Francis Schaeffer

R.C. Sproul

About This Book

This book is the result of the labors Roger Ellsworth and his wife, Sylvia, and the thought they have given to various passages of Scripture over the years. You may read more about Roger and Sylvia on page 141.

We hope you will enjoy these Bible-based meditations. We would love to hear from you, so please send us a note to tell us what you think—which ones you liked most, and how they made a difference in your life or in the life of a family member, friend, or work associate. To reach us online, go to
www.mycoffeecupmeditations.com/contact

Table of Contents

1 Old Houses, New Houses 16
2 The Faith Chapter 20
3 The Hope Chapter 24
4 The Love Chapter 28
5 Three Cheers from Jesus 32
6 From Lucifer to Satan 36
7 The Bible in the Toilet 40
8 Heavy Truth from Henry Lyte 44
9 Ministers and Materials 48
10 Unable and Able 52
11 Anticipation (A Reading from Sylvia) 56
12 The Bible's Tragic Figures: Cain 60
13 The Bible's Tragic Figures: Esau 64
14 The Bible's Tragic Figures: The Elders of Israel 68
15 The Bible's Tragic Figures: King Saul 72
16 The Bible's Tragic Figures: Amaziah 76
17 The Bible's Tragic Figures: Judas 80
18 The Hymn of the Three C's 84
19 An Old Man with a Flat Tire 88
20 Dr. Brown's Body 92
21 Pushing the Pool or Moving the Bucket 96
22 From Riches to Poverty to Riches (A Reading from Sylvia) 100
23 Simple Song, Sublime Truth 104
24 I Am Resolved 108
25 The Voice of Christ 112

26 The Word and Prayer 116
27 Living a "ful"er Life (1) 120
28 Living a "ful"er Life (2) 124
29 Are You a Theophilus? 128
30 What is the Evidence for Jesus? 132
31 "'Till We Meet Again" (A Reading from Sylvia) 136

About the Authors 141
The Series 142

The App

www.mycoffeecupmeditations.com

Be sure you get the app!

-1-

From God's Word, the Bible...

"In My Father's house are many mansions; if it were not so, I would have told you. I go to prepare a place for you."

For we know that if our earthly house, this tent, is destroyed, we have a building from God, a house not made with hands, eternal in the heavens.

John 14:2; 2 Corinthians 5:1

Old Houses, New Houses

It was finally gone, the victim of the cold steel of a bulldozer's blade. I knew the end was rapidly approaching, but I still hated to see it go.

I'm talking about the little old house in which I spent the first twenty-one years of my life. Little? Yes. It consisted of a kitchen, a living room, two bedrooms, a pantry, and a porch. Oh, yes, there was also that little area on one side that my mother referred to as "the sun room."

What about the bathroom? There was no bathroom. We used the privy, which was situated a little way down the hill. My folks, you see, were very poor. We just had enough money, as they put it, "to make ends meet."

The old house was in bad condition all through my young years. Walking across the floor would cause it to sort of creak and groan as if it were offering a protest against the person who was adding more weight to its weary existence. The walls were adorned with various cracks and holes. And the foundation could only see its sturdy days in the rear-view mirror.

But I loved that old house. It wasn't the physical structure that made it lovable. It was rather what went on there. The love and respect we had for each other, the happiness and the laughter, the gratitude we felt for the Lord's blessings, and our shared faith in the precious gospel of Christ—all of these things and many more made the old house a palace of delight.

One of the most pleasant memories of my childhood is my mother filling that old house with singing before Parkinson's disease made her body like the house itself—weak, weary, and worn.

I treasure the lessons that I learned in my years in the old house, one of which was that it isn't necessary to have lots of money to be rich. Greater still was this lesson: believers in Christ have two new houses awaiting them. One is a new body. Paul says we have "a building from God, a house not made with hands, eternal in the heavens" (2 Cor. 5:1). My body is an "earthly house," a "tent," which will be "destroyed." But when Jesus comes I will receive a new body (Phil. 3:20-21).

The second house believers will receive is the "Father's house" (John 14:1). That term is Jesus' shorthand for our eternal home that is so beautifully described for us in Revelation 21 and 22.

Here, then, is the final outcome for believers in Christ—we will live in new bodies on a new earth. Those bodies will be beyond the reach of disease and death. No Parkinson's in heaven, and no death either! Thank God! And the new earth will be beyond the reach of sin and Satan. The Apostle Peter refers to it as "an inheritance" that is "incorruptible and undefiled." He also says that it "does not fade away," but it is "reserved in heaven" for us (1 Peter 1:4).

Christians have indescribable glory awaiting them, and

it's all because of the Lord Jesus Christ. He came from heaven's glory to this earth to take us from this earth to heaven's glory.

When will believers in Christ receive their new houses? When Jesus comes! One glorious day, He will break through the clouds "with a shout, with the voice of an archangel, and with the trumpet of God" (1 Thess. 4:16). Dead believers will hear the voice of their Lord, and they will spring from their graves in marvelous resurrection life. Living believers will be "caught up" (1 Thess. 4:17). They will instantaneously receive their new bodies without having to pass through death. And then the Lord will escort all of His people to their new house in heaven. New bodies on a new earth—what a destiny!

As we wait for the glory of that day, we live in this world of change and decay. Nothing here lasts. How thankful we should be that we have the Lord to abide with us! Before her disease took her voice, my mother used to sing:

> *Swift to its close ebbs out life's little day;*
> *Earth's joys grow dim, its glories pass away;*
> *Change and decay in all around I see:*
> *O Thou who changest not, abide with me!*
> (Henry F. Lyte)

-2-

From God's Word, the Bible...

*Now faith is the substance of things hoped for,
the evidence of things not seen.*

Hebrews 11:1

The Faith Chapter

Faith, hope, and love are often linked together in Scripture. It is interesting that one chapter of Scripture is devoted to each of these graces. Romans 8 is the hope chapter; 1 Corinthians 13 is the love chapter; and Hebrews 11 is the faith chapter.

The author writes: "Now faith is the substance of things hoped for, the evidence of things not seen" (v. 1). In other words, faith is the assurance that the things God has promised are true and certain. It treats them as being solid and real even though they are at this time unseen and unfulfilled. John Calvin says faith gives the believer "a sure and secure possession of those things which God has promised."

The New International Version translates verse 1 in this way: "Now faith is being sure of what we hope for and certain of what we do not see."

The author himself further defines faith as he makes reference to the great heroes of the faith: "These all died in faith, not having received the promises, but having seen them afar off were assured of them, embraced them, and confessed that they were strangers and pilgrims on the earth" (v. 12).

Many mistake faith for mere positive thinking. They think faith is selecting something we want to be true and convincing ourselves that it will be true. But that's not faith. Faith is rather believing what God has said. Faith cannot function in a vacuum. It functions on the basis of the Word of God (Rom. 10:17). Faith is sure because God has promised.

When we go through the list of the men and women of faith that the author of Hebrews mentions, we see that each one believed something that God had revealed.

Think about Abel (v. 4). Before he was born, God revealed the kind of sacrifice that was acceptable to Him, namely, a blood sacrifice (Gen. 3:21). Undoubtedly, Abel learned about this revelation from his parents, accepted it and acted on the basis of it.

Then there's Noah (v. 7), who was told by God that the flood was going to come on the earth. He believed this revelation and built the ark.

Abraham (vv. 8-10) was told by God to leave his homeland and go to a new country (Gen. 12:1-4), and he acted on the basis of that word. He also received from God the revelation that the future holds for believers something far better than anything this life has to offer, that is, "the city which has foundations, whose builder and maker is God" (v. 10). Abraham also believed that promise and eagerly looked forward to its fulfillment.

Sarah (vv. 11-12) and Abraham received from God the definite promise that she would conceive and bear a son in her old age, and this son would be the one through whom the promises God made to Abraham would be fulfilled (Gen. 18:9-15). The fact that Sarah laughed when she heard this promise indicates that one can have real faith and still waver. Weak faith is still faith.

The greatest test of Abraham's faith came when God

commanded him to sacrifice Isaac (vv. 17-19). Abraham knew that Isaac had to survive because God had clearly said: "In Isaac your seed shall be called" (v. 18; Gen. 21:12), and at this point Isaac himself had no children.

Because Abraham knew Isaac had to survive, he concluded that if he indeed had to sacrifice Isaac, God would have to raise him from the dead (v. 19). God, of course, provided a ram for Abraham to sacrifice instead of Isaac (Gen. 22:13). God's purpose in all this was to point Abraham and Isaac ahead to the redeeming death of the Lord Jesus Christ.

Moses (vv. 23-29), knowing that God had promised to deliver the people of Israel from bondage in Egypt, left his life in Egypt behind and identified himself with the people of God (vv. 24-27). After receiving clear instructions from God, he led the people of Israel in the observance of the Passover (v. 28) and also across the Red Sea (v. 29).

All these heroes of the faith join their voices to urge us to believe the Word of God, no matter how foolish it may seem to do so. And they also remind us that while true faith may struggle and waver, it can never be extinguished.

The Bible emphasizes that faith—saving faith—is always to be put in the Lord Jesus Christ. He is the great Savior of sinners. Each of the people in today's reading looked ahead to the coming of the One whom God had appointed to live and die in their place—and to rise again as the Lord, victorious over death. Is your faith in Him alone?

-3-

From God's Word, the Bible...

For we were saved in this hope, but hope that is seen is not hope; for why does one still hope for what he sees? But if we hope for what we do not see, we eagerly wait for it with perseverance.

Romans 8:24-25

The Hope Chapter

Romans 8 is the hope chapter of the Bible. While the word "hope" itself is mentioned only six times in its thirty-nine verses, the theme of hope permeates almost the entire chapter.

Paul asserts that Christians are saved in hope (v. 24). When Christians are saved, they are placed in the realm of hope. They live out the remainder of their lives in that realm.

That won't seem to be such a great thing if we fail to understand the meaning of hope. To us, hope conveys possible doubt or uncertainty. Someone says he is hoping to get a good report from the doctor. The person who says that isn't sure; the report may be good or bad.

We sometimes hear people say this: "All we can do is hope for the best." That phrase is often used in serious situations in which the outcome is in doubt. We also hear people say: "Hope for the best and expect the worst." That means the outcome of a particular situation is up in the air.

Our modern use of the word "hope" is not the same as that of the Bible. To us, hope is weak. In the Bible, it is strong. We will understand hope better if we place it alongside faith. Faith is the calm assurance that all the things that God has promised will prove to be true. It views them as being solid and real even though they are now unseen and unfulfilled. Faith is certainty.

In the Bible, hope goes beyond faith. Faith says: "I am sure this will happen." Hope says: "I can't wait to see it." Hope is eager expectation. It is the believer standing on tiptoe and craning his neck to see that thing which faith makes him or her certain of.

In Romans 8, the Apostle Paul mentions two things that the Christian is ever so eager to see. One is the redemption of all creation (vv. 18-22); the other is the redemption of the body (vv. 23-25).

In my years as a pastor, I was often surprised to discover that many churchgoers seem to have little or no understanding of the redemption of creation.

The natural realm is not as God made it. All of creation fell when Adam fell. Paul refers to it as being "subjected to futility, not willingly" (v. 20). Through no fault of its own, creation was seriously damaged by human sin. Paul also refers to it as being in "bondage" (v. 21).

That is not the final word for this natural order. Paul tells us that this earth is eagerly awaiting "the glorious liberty of the children of God" (v. 21) because it will share in that liberty. Creation itself will finally be delivered from its fallen condition. When the end comes, it will be restored to its original beauty and glory. God's work of salvation consists of Him restoring what Satan has ruined. That includes this earth. If God doesn't put the earth back to where it was before sin entered, Satan will have won a tremendous victory.

The other thing that the Christian is eager to see is the redemption of the body.

Just as creation was affected by sin, so was the human

body. It is so feeble and frail and prone to disease. All of this is the result of sin. So as creation groans in anticipation of its redemption, so we groan within ourselves as we wait for the redemption of our bodies.

When a Christian dies, the soul immediately goes to be with the Lord and the body goes into the grave. There the body will remain until Jesus comes. When He comes, He will bring with Him the souls of all dead believers, will raise their bodies from their graves, and reunite souls and bodies. On that day, Jesus won't merely resuscitate our bodies so we can resume life as we knew it before. It will be so we can begin a whole new kind of existence. We will have bodies like the resurrection body of Jesus, and in those bodies we will live on the earth that has itself been redeemed (Phil. 3:20-21; 1 Thess. 4:13-18; 1 John 3:1-2).

A new body on a new earth! This is the glorious future of the Christian!

And it is all because of the redeeming work of Christ. Each believer should look back on His life and death with great gratitude and look forward to the future, saying: "Bring it on! I can't wait to see it!"

-4-

From God's Word, the Bible...

Though I speak with the tongues of men and of angels, but have not love, I have become sounding brass or a clanging cymbal.

1 Corinthians 13:1

The Love Chapter

There's no debate that 1 Corinthians 13 is the love chapter of the Bible. In beautiful and moving words, Paul calls the believers in Corinth away from their fascination with spiritual gifts to the higher priority of love. It is, in the words of Paul, "a more excellent way" (12:31).

What is love? It is having such a strong affection for others that we give ourselves to doing that which is in their best interest.

In verses 4-7, Paul lays out fifteen characteristics of love. When we see someone demonstrating these characteristics we are seeing that person practicing or manifesting love. Paul tells us that love:

- suffers long—it's slow to anger as it puts up with that which is unpleasant and distasteful in other people;
- is kind—it is gracious and tender, like the Lord Jesus;
- doesn't envy—it isn't unhappy when others succeed;
- doesn't parade itself—it doesn't allow us to live for notice and applause;

- isn't puffed up—it doesn't allow us to be so full of ourselves that we act arrogantly and talk conceitedly;
- doesn't behave rudely—it's so gentle and sensitive that it refuses to do things that bring shame or embarrassment to others;
- doesn't seek its own—it doesn't insist on its own way but constantly insists on seeking the wellbeing of others;
- isn't provoked—it's not irritable, temperamental, touchy, thin-skinned, or easily offended;
- thinks no evil—it doesn't keep a record of wrongs;
- doesn't rejoice in iniquity—it doesn't receive pleasure from the failures and misfortunes of others;
- rejoices in the truth—it is always happy to see the truth win;
- bears all things—it passes over in silence and keeps confidential that which is repugnant in others;
- believes all things—it's always ready to see the best in others and to give them the benefit of the doubt;
- hopes all things—it isn't pessimistic about those who have been troublesome in the past, that is, it doesn't easily give up on others;
- endures all things—it refuses to be dismayed and conquered.

Why did Paul go into such detail to describe love? He wanted his readers to see that *love outperforms all the spiritual gifts*. It's possible to have spiritual gifts without demonstrating these wonderful qualities, but it's not possible to have love without demonstrating them.

Paul closes the chapter with another emphasis—*love outlasts the gifts* (vv. 8-13). The Apostle points his readers to the coming of "that which is perfect" (v. 10), that is, to the coming of the perfect eternal day when believers in Christ will see

God face to face and all things will be made clear (v. 12). On that day, all partial things will be put away (v. 10) because that which is partial is not perfect.

The putting away of partial things will mean the putting away of the gifts. Prophecy, tongues, and knowledge (the ability to grasp and communicate God's Word in a special way) will have no place in heaven. But when the gifts are gone, the graces will abide. We will exercise faith in heaven as we continue to depend on God to provide for us. We will exercise hope in heaven as we eagerly look forward to discovering more of its treasures. But while faith and hope will be in heaven, they will not surpass love.

Why will love be greater in heaven than faith and hope? It makes us like God. God doesn't have faith or hope, but He is love.

In Paul's list of love's qualities, we see the Lord Jesus, who is the only person who has ever perfectly practiced them. We should know that we will never be able to perfectly practice true love in this life as He did. We should also know that we should be ever striving to follow His example. We don't really have Him as our example if we haven't taken Him as our Lord and Savior.

To love as God loves, we must know God through repenting of our sins and trusting in His Son. The Apostle John says: "Beloved, let us love one another, for love is of God, and everyone who loves is born of God and knows God. . . . In this is love, not that we loved God, but that He loved us and sent His Son to be the propitiation for our sins" (1 John 4:7,10).

-5-

From God's Word, the Bible...

So He got into a boat, crossed over, and came to His own city. Then behold, they brought to Him a paralytic lying on a bed. When Jesus saw their faith, He said to the paralytic, "Son, be of good cheer; your sins are forgiven you."

But Jesus turned around, and when He saw her He said, "Be of good cheer, daughter; your faith has made you well." And the woman was made well from that hour.

But immediately Jesus spoke to them, saying, "Be of good cheer! It is I; do not be afraid."

Matthew 9:1-2,22; 14:27

Three Cheers from Jesus

The Gospel of Matthew reports three occasions on which Jesus said: "Be of good cheer." On each of those occasions, Jesus was speaking to an individual or a group who were beaten down and on the verge of despair.

On the first occasion, Jesus spoke to a man who had been paralyzed for a long time. On the second occasion, He spoke to a woman who for twelve years had suffered from a hemorrhage. On the third occasion, He spoke to His disciples who were trying to pilot their little boat through a stormy sea.

What are the truths that we can draw from these situations? The first is this: *We can be of good cheer because Jesus forgives sin* (9:1-2).

In this passage we have a paralyzed man lying on his bed, and Jesus says: "Be of good cheer; your sins are forgiven you."

What does this say to us? The answer couldn't be plainer. It affirms that Jesus regarded this man's spiritual condition as being more important than his physical condition. That's not to say that Jesus wasn't interested in his physical condition. He was, and He proved it by healing him. But that's not where Jesus started. No one had said a word to Jesus about forgiving this man's sins, but that is where Jesus began.

Jesus put the emphasis in the right place. We all have to leave this world and meet God. No one will be able to stand in God's holy presence unless his sins are forgiven. The good news that emerges from Jesus' dealings with the paralyzed man is this: Jesus can and does forgive sins. He came to this earth for the express purpose of providing the way for our sins to be forgiven. He did so by dying on the cross. There He received the penalty for sinners so that all who come to Him in repentance and faith will never receive that same penalty but will rather receive forgiveness.

The second truth we see from the three cheers of Jesus is this: *We can be of good cheer because Jesus values imperfect faith* (9:22).

The woman who had suffered for twelve years with "a flow of blood" (9:20) quite obviously had imperfect faith. Her faith that Jesus could heal her was mixed up with some superstition. She seems to have regarded Jesus as something of a magician who exuded power to those who touched Him. So, she managed to work her way through the crowd around Jesus and touch Him. And that touch was rewarded as Jesus healed her.

We can and should be thankful that the Lord doesn't require us to have perfect faith before He saves us. Weak faith is still faith. What a consolation that is! J.C. Ryle writes:

> Our faith may be feeble; our courage may be small; our grasp of the Gospel and its promises, may be weak and trembling, —but, after all, the grand question is, Do we

really trust only in Christ? Do we look to Jesus, and only to Jesus, for pardon and peace? If this be so, it is well.[1]

The truth we discover from Jesus' third cheering statement is very comforting, namely, *We can be of good cheer because Jesus is with us in the storms of life* (14:27).

After feeding a multitude of five thousand, Jesus told His disciples to cross the Sea of Galilee. They soon encountered a ferocious storm. The boat "was now in the middle of the sea, tossed by waves, for the wind was contrary" (14:24).

Jesus came to His disciples by walking on the sea. His first words to them were: "Be of good cheer! It is I; do not be afraid."

Jesus did marvelous things in that storm. He enabled Simon Peter to walk toward Him on the water and then rescued him when, after a good start, he began to sink. Jesus then stepped with Simon into the boat, and the wind immediately ceased (14:28-32).

We have our storms, too. And they can be very threatening and frightening. But the Lord Jesus has promised to be with us all through this life (Heb. 13:5), and that includes the storms. With Him beside us, our fear can give away to cheer.

These three passages put the Lord Jesus on display. We see His perfect knowledge, His abounding sympathy, and His sovereign authority and power. Our response should be to worship Him as His disciples did when He stilled the storm (14:33).

---

[1] J.C. Ryle, *Expository Thoughts on Matthew*, The Banner of Truth Trust, Edinburgh, 1995, p. 89.

-6-

From God's Word, the Bible...

We know that we are of God, and the whole world lies under the sway of the wicked one.
And we know that the Son of God has come and has given us an understanding, that we may know Him who is true; and we are in Him who is true, in His Son Jesus Christ.
This is the true God and eternal life.

1 John 5:19-20

From Lucifer to Satan

The name "Satan" means "adversary." There is a real person that the Bible calls "Satan." He is the adversary of God and of the people of God. He hates each with equal passion. Where did Satan come from? He didn't start out as Satan. Far from it! He started out as Lucifer, which means "morning star" or "day star." He was one of the many angels that God created to serve Him. But it's not enough to say that he was one of the angels. He was supreme among the angels as these words indicate:

You were the seal of perfection,
Full of wisdom and perfect in beauty...
You were the anointed cherub who covers...
You were perfect in your ways from the day you were created....
(Ezek. 28:12,14,15)

Jonathan Edwards understood the phrase "the anointed cherub that covers" to indicate that Lucifer enjoyed special status in heaven, standing next to the very throne of God.

Edwards writes:

> ...before the fall of this cherub he is spoken of as being alone entitled to this great honour and nearness to God's throne in heaven, that he was anointed to be above his fellows.[2]

But Lucifer didn't retain his exalted name and position. He became Satan. How did he go from morning star to adversary? The Bible answers by telling us Lucifer developed "I" trouble. Notice how he uses the word "I" five times in Isaiah 14:13-14.

> *I will ascend into heaven,*
> *I will exalt my throne above the stars of God;*
> *I will also sit on the mount of the congregation.*
> *I will ascend above the heights of the clouds,*
> *I will be like the Most High.*
> (Isa. 14:13-14)

The first sin that ever occurred was not when Adam and Eve disobeyed God in the Garden of Eden. It took place in the heart of Lucifer before this world was created. It was pride.

I have to connect the sin of Lucifer with God's plan of redemption. We know that plan was put in place before the world began. God knew that He would create this world as well as Adam and Eve. He also knew that Adam and Eve would fall into sin. So before there was a world and before there was a man, God put in place His marvelous plan of salvation. The three persons of the Trinity developed this plan in which each would play a part. The centerpiece of this plan

---

[2] Jonathan Edwards, *The Works of Jonathan Edwards* (Edinburgh, UK: The Banner of Truth Trust, 1988), vol. ii, p.609.

was the Son coming to this earth in our humanity, living in perfect obedience to God, dying on the cross, and rising again.

That plan was not only formulated in heaven. It was also announced in heaven. The angels were told that the Son would step into this earth as a man and that they would have to worship and serve Him in His humanity as well as minister to human beings.

That was too much for Lucifer. His pride wouldn't allow him to serve the Son in human form and other human beings. That was beneath him! Jonathan Edwards writes of Lucifer:

> But when it was revealed to him, high and glorious as he was, that he must be a ministering spirit to the race of mankind which he had seen newly created, which appeared so feeble, mean, and despicable, so vastly inferior, ... he could not bear it. This occasioned his fall. . . .[3]

Dissatisfied with God's plan, Lucifer made a plan of his own. He would overthrow God and take His place. Although he was joined in his rebellion by one third of all the angels (Rev. 12:4), the whole enterprise came crashing down. Lucifer and his followers were expelled from heaven (Rev. 12:7-9).

Lucifer's plan failed and God's plan went forward. But Satan is still alive, and he is still opposing God and God's people. Why does God allow him to do so? We don't have all the answers we would like. We have to wait for those. Instead of dwelling on what we don't know, we should dwell on what we do know—God is greater than Satan. He defeated him when he first rebelled. He defeated him again when Jesus died on the cross (Col. 2:15). And He will defeat him yet again at the end of human history (Rev. 20:10).

---

[3] Edwards, vol. ii, p.610.

-7-

From God's Word, the Bible...

Forever, O L<small>ORD</small>,
Your word is settled in heaven.

Psalm 119:89

The Bible in the Toilet

I had placed my Bible on a table in the church foyer a few minutes before our evening worship service was to begin. But when I went back, it was gone. I asked a couple of the church members if they knew what happened to my Bible. It was then that I learned that two young men had come into the church. It soon became clear that they weren't there to worship but rather to ridicule and threaten. They were invited to stay for the service, but they refused to do so, and parted with a few comments about how stupid all of us were to believe and practice what they referred to as "this stuff."

They were gone and my Bible was gone. Had they taken it with them? Several people fanned out across the building to look for the missing Bible. One of the men soon returned to say he had found it. It was stuffed in the toilet in the men's room.

Having attended a secular university, I was used to being around Christian-haters, but I was still a little surprised at what these young ruffians had done with my Bible. That was a long time ago. Hatred of Christianity has grown so much the last several years that I wouldn't be surprised at all if the same thing were to happen to me today.

The prophet Jeremiah had an experience similar to mine. We read about it in Jeremiah 36. The Lord commanded Jeremiah to write on a scroll the words that He, the Lord, had given Jeremiah to speak (v. 1).

We have in this command a small picture of how the whole Bible came to exist. God prompted men to write what He wanted written (2 Tim. 3:16; 2 Peter 1:21).

When the scroll was completed, it was read at the temple "in the hearing of all the people" (v. 10). It was then read to the princes of the kingdom. These men were filled with fear as they listened to this reading because Jeremiah's scroll contained the message of God's judgment (vv. 11-19).

These princes decided that the scroll should be read to King Jehoiakim, who was sitting "in the winter house in the ninth month, with a fire burning on the hearth before him" (v. 22).

Jehoiakim's response to this is shocking: he listened to part of the reading and then "cut it with the scribe's knife and cast it into the fire that was on the hearth" (v. 23).

The princes who had wanted the scroll read to the king were astonished at the attitude of the king and his attendants. The king had burned the scroll, which was presented to him as God's Word, but the king and his attendants "were not afraid, nor did they tear their garments" (v. 24).

The king even went so far as to command that Jeremiah and his secretary, Baruch, be arrested (v. 26). Such was his disdain for the Word of God and the men of God!

Jeremiah's Bible in the fire and mine in the toilet—sad ends for those copies of God's Word! But while men can destroy copies of God's Word, they can never destroy God's

Word. The truth of this is brought out in powerful fashion by the remaining verses of Jeremiah 36. After the king burned the first scroll, the Lord said to Jeremiah: "Take yet another scroll, and write on it all the former words that were in the first scroll which Jehoiakim the king of Judah has burned" (v. 28).

Would Jeremiah be able to remember all that was in the burned scroll? Perhaps not, but the Lord has no trouble with His memory! So, the second scroll perfectly repeated the words of the first and also included "many similar words" (v. 32).

Jehoiakim paid a fearful price for casting God's Word into the fire. It caused him to experience the fire of God's judgment (v. 30). He comes to us from the Scripture he hated so much to tell us that we can't finally destroy God's Word, but it can destroy us.

What about the young men who destroyed my Bible? I don't know what became of them. They may now be out in eternity. I can only hope that they came to see the folly of their contempt for God's Word and began to treasure it.

And what about the Bible? I have a copy right here beside me.

-8-

From God's Word, the Bible...

Yet indeed I also count all things loss for the excellence of the knowledge of Christ Jesus my Lord, for whom I have suffered the loss of all things, and count them as rubbish, that I may gain Christ. . . .

Philippians 3:8

Heavy Truth from Henry Lyte

Henry Lyte was a wonderful trophy for the grace of God. Born on June 1, 1793, in Scotland, Henry entered the ministry in 1815. While engaged in ministering to others, Henry himself had not truly come to the knowledge of Christ. That would soon change. In 1816, he visited a dying priest who said that he and Henry had been wrong in not interpreting the epistles of Paul "in their plain and literal sense."

That comment prompted Henry to study the Bible more thoroughly and carefully, and that study led to his conversion.

Henry Lyte became a powerful preacher and hymnwriter. The best known of his hymns is *Abide With Me*. But he also wrote *Jesus, I My Cross Have Taken*.

This hymn has brought blessing to me. It is the hymn of one who had determined to follow the Lord no matter how great the cost. In the first verse of the hymn, Henry addresses the Lord.

> *Jesus, I my cross have taken,*
> *All to leave and follow Thee;*
> *Destitute, despised, forsaken,*
> *Thou, from hence, my all shalt be.*

In the second verse, Henry seems to speak to himself:

> *Perish every fond ambition,*
> *All I've sought, and hoped, and known;*
> *Yet how rich is my condition,*
> *God and Christ are still my own.*

It's plain that Henry scorned the notion of a cheap, easy Christianity that requires nothing and can just be tacked on to our lives as one more interest among several others. If Christianity is not the main thing to us, is it anything at all? The Lord was so important to Henry Lyte that he was willing to give up everything for Him. To those who would exclaim, "Poor Henry," he says: "Yet how rich is my condition." Those who have made Christ their all are never the worse for the bargain!

He knew how to value things. He goes on to say to God:

> *And, while Thou shalt smile upon me,*
> *God of wisdom, love, and might,*
> *Foes may hate, and friends disown me;*
> *Show Thy face, and all is bright.*

In the last verse, Henry again addresses himself:

> *Haste then on from grace to glory,*
> *Armed by faith and winged by prayer;*
> *God's eternal day's before thee,*
> *God's own hand shall guide thee there.*

Soon shall close thy earthly mission,
Swift shall pass thy pilgrim days,
Hope shall change to glad fruition,
Faith to sight, and prayer to praise.

There's so much in those lines to challenge and cheer the hearts of believers in Christ. Here's a cheerful thought: we are journeying from grace to glory. It's God grace that makes us Christians, and that grace will not finish with us until it finally deposits us in the glory of heaven.

Here's a challenging thought: we are to be "armed by faith and winged by prayer." Faith is a matter of degrees. Every Christian has faith, and every Christian needs more faith. Faith arms us. It enables us to stand strong against the devil and all his devices. And every Christian needs to be more engaged in prayer. It gives us wings. It is the way we soar aloft to the Lord in heaven.

Here's another cheerful thought: while we wait for God's eternal day to dawn, we have His guiding hand to lead us along.

And here's another challenging thought: our earthly mission shall soon close and our pilgrim days shall soon pass. We need to be about the Master's business. As wonderful as heaven will be, it will not give us the opportunity to do what we should have done while on this earth.

Henry himself got a lot of dedication to the Lord out of his life even though he was plagued with ill health for most of it. He finally entered the presence of the Lord he loved on November 20, 1847.

I'm thankful for this hymn. It makes me realize that I need to be more dedicated and determined in my service to the Lord. When this great hymn comes to mind, I invariably say this: while his name was Lyte, his hymn was heavy with truth.

-9-

From God's Word, the Bible...

According to the grace of God which was given to me, as a wise master builder I have laid the foundation, and another builds on it. But let each one take heed how he builds on it.

1 Corinthians 3:10

Ministers and Materials

Much of what Paul has to say in the early chapters of 1 Corinthians has to do with the gospel ministry. That is still his dominant emphasis in the third chapter of this epistle. He identifies Apollos and himself as "ministers" that the Lord had used to bring the Corinthians to faith in Christ (v. 5).

From that point he proceeds to picture Apollos and himself as farmers (vv. 6-8) and himself as a builder (vv. 10-17) with the church at Corinth being their field and his building (v. 9).

Paul leaves Apollos out when he, Paul, talks about himself as a builder. The reason is that Paul was the one who had laid the foundation for the church in Corinth, and he wanted to define the gospel ministry in terms of that foundation.

What was the foundation that Paul had put in place in Corinth? It was the Lord Jesus Christ (v. 10). Paul knew that other ministers would be coming into Corinth, and he wanted to warn his readers to make sure that those ministers of the future would not depart from the foundation that he himself had laid.

The true minister recognizes that it is not his job to lay a foundation for the church. That has already been done. It is now his responsibility to decide what kind of material he is going to use in building on that foundation (v. 12).

What are the materials that the minister has at his disposal? Paul pictures them as gold, silver, precious stones, wood, hay, and straw (v. 12).

It's plain that those six materials fall into two categories. The gold, silver, and precious stones are in the valuable and lasting category. The wood, hay, and straw are in the worthless and perishable category.

We must understand that Paul wasn't using these materials in a physical sense but in a spiritual sense. He was using them to picture the way the church must be built up spiritually. These materials represent the teachings or the doctrines that the minister uses to build the church. The gold, silver, and precious stones are those doctrines that best correspond to the foundation. The wood, hay, and straw represent teachings that don't correspond to the foundation.

The foundation is a gospel foundation. It consists of the redeeming work of Christ. The gold, silver, and precious stones are those teachings that set forth the work of Christ. They wood, hay. and straw are those teachings that depart from the work of Christ to offer cheap and vain substitutes.

We don't have to look very far to see that Paul's words about the ministry are just as important today as they were when he wrote them. Gold, silver, and precious stones seem to be coming from pulpits more and more infrequently. But wood, hay, and straw are being offered and heard again and again.

Where is the gold of the Lord of Glory coming to this earth in our humanity to rescue those who trust in Him from the horrible consequences of their sins? Where is the silver of His sinless life and His substitutionary death on the cross? Where are the precious stones of His resurrection from the grave and His ascension to heaven from which He poured out on His church the gift of the Holy Spirit?

Where are those preachers who preach the gospel "by the Holy Spirit sent from heaven" (1 Peter 1:12)? Where are those who feel the weight of standing before eternity-bound people? Yes, they can still be found, but they are not as numerous as they once were. In their places, we have chuckling jokesters who are more like entertainers and performers than gospel ministers.

Everyone who dares to preach should never stand before a congregation without thinking of the fearful day of exposure that is coming. Ministers and ministries will eventually be tested by the fire that "will test each one's work" to determine "of what sort it is" (v. 13).

What a sorrowful thing it will be for ministers to have revealed to the whole universe that their ministries were worthless because those ministries weren't Christ-centered! On the other hand, what a blessing it will be for ministers to finally see their Christ-centered ministries honored and rewarded (v. 14)!

Paul's words ought to cause each of us to realize how vital true gospel ministry is. If we aren't under such a ministry, we should seek it. If we are, we should prize it.

-10-

From God's Word, the Bible...

"I am not able to bear all these people alone, because the burden is too heavy for me."

. . . so Christ was offered once to bear the sins of many. To those who eagerly wait for Him He will appear a second time, apart from sin, for salvation.

. . . who Himself bore our sins in His own body on the tree, that we, having died to sins, might live for righteousness—by whose stripes you were healed.

Numbers 11:14; Hebrews 9:28; 1 Peter 2:24

Unable and Able

One of my elementary-school teachers seemed to take delight in lecturing us on the proper usage of the words "can" and "may." There was a pencil sharpener stationed on her desk, but we weren't to use it during class time without her permission. Invariably, one of my classmates would raise his or her hand and say: "Can I please use the pencil sharpener?" And our teacher would invariably respond: "I don't know. Can you?" And then she would launch into this explanation:

"'Can' is a word of ability. When you ask if you can use the pencil sharpener, you're asking if you have the ability to use it, and I think you probably do have that ability. I think you possess the ability to walk forward, insert the pencil in the sharpener, and turn the crank. The word 'may' is the word you should use. It is a word of permission. You have the ability to use the sharpener. What you're asking for is my permission."

Moses knew how to use the words "can" and "can't." In Numbers 11:14, he says to the Lord: "I am not able to bear all these people alone, because the burden is too heavy for me."

He was saying: "I can't." He was saying: "I don't have the ability."

I can understand Moses' exasperation. He was in the process of leading the Israelites from crushing slavery in Egypt to freedom in their own land, the land of Canaan. One would think that those people would have been a happy, grateful lot—happy to be out of Egypt, and grateful to Moses. Someone has observed that we can go through life being humbly grateful or grumbly hateful. Many of these Israelites fell into the latter category. Instead of being thankful for the manna that the Lord provided for them, they complained and craved meat (vv. 4-6).

They were fed up with the manna, and Moses was fed up with them. They complained to Moses, and he complained to the Lord (vv. 10-15).

Moses was at his wits' end. He had reached his breaking point. That's when he essentially said to the Lord: "I can't do it any longer. I don't have the ability to put up with them any longer."

I try to never read Moses' words without thinking of the Lord Jesus Christ. The work of redemption for sinners would require Jesus to "bear" their sins. It would require Him to come to this earth in our humanity and go the cross to receive the penalty that our sins deserve. That penalty was nothing less than the wrath of God. When the Father set that work before His Son way back there in eternity past, thank God, the Son didn't say: "I can't do it." He rather said: "I can do it." And I think He also must have said: "I will do it."

So He came to this earth as a man. He lived in perfect obedience to God. He died on the cross. He arose from the grave and ascended to the Father in heaven. When it was all done, he added to His "I can" and "I will" these words: "I have." He had the ability to do the work. He was determined to do the work. And He did the work.

The main part of His saving work was His death on the cross. How very thankful we should be for that cross! There Jesus "was offered once to bear the sins of many" (Heb. 9:28). There "He Himself bore our sins in His own body" (1 Peter 2:24).

Jesus could bear our sins, and He did bear them. So we now rejoice in Him.

There was One Who was willing to die in my stead,
That a soul so unworthy might live;
And the path to the cross He was willing to tread,
All the sins of my life to forgive.

They are nailed to the cross! They are nailed to the cross!
Oh, how much He was willing to bear!
With what anguish and loss Jesus went to the cross,
But He carried my sins with Him there.
(Carrie A. Breck)

-11-

From God's Word, the Bible...

For our citizenship is in heaven, from which we also eagerly wait for the Savior, the Lord Jesus Christ....

...looking for the blessed hope and glorious appearing of our great God and Savior Jesus Christ....

Philippians 3:20; Titus 2:13

Anticipation

A Reading from Sylvia

Life is filled with much anticipation. Children look forward to Christmas with eager anticipation. Teenagers anticipate getting their driver's licenses. Even though fifty years have passed, I still remember how much Roger and I anticipated our wedding day.

One of my earliest memories involves anticipation. I was three years old. My parents were married during World War II. They lived near the naval base on the west coast where my father's ship was undergoing repairs. They were only married a few weeks until he was shipped out. Mother returned to her parents' home halfway across the country to await his return. That return never happened. He was killed a few weeks after their parting when his ship was attacked by the Japanese.

Shortly after her return home, Mother discovered she was pregnant, and I was born a few months after my father's death. Six months after I was born, my grandfather died, so Mother and I continued to live with my grandmother.

Mother got a job, and Grandma took care of me when Mother was at work.

Now back to that anticipation thing. We lived a couple of miles from town. Every afternoon when it was about time for Mother to arrive home from work, Grandma would take me out to the enclosed front porch with windows on three sides. From there, we could see a long distance down the road in the direction Mother would be coming from town. I remember a small hill far in the distance. Grandma would tell me to watch for Mother's car to appear over the crest of that hill. Oh, how I would keep my eyes glued to that hill as I eagerly anticipated the sight of Mother's car! I had no doubt that she would indeed be coming over that hill.

The anticipation I felt in those childhood days is a faint picture of that which all of us who know the Lord should experience as we await His return and anticipate our heavenly home. Paul urged the Corinthians to be "eagerly waiting for the revelation of our Lord Jesus Christ" (1 Cor. 1:7).

I eagerly anticipate things I know will not be in heaven such as sin, sickness, sorrow, tears, separations, and death. None of these things will ever touch us again.

I eagerly anticipate things that must surely be part of heaven:

- Seeing the Lord Jesus Christ and worshiping Him. Every sight of His nail-scarred hands will be a reminder of the sacrifice that made heaven possible for us and will stir within us more praise and love for our Savior.
- Uncovering layer after layer of who God is and all He has done. With each discovery will come a greater depth of praise and worship.
- Discovering all the ways God protected and guided us throughout our lives when we weren't even aware of it.
- Being reunited with our believing loved ones.

- Meeting and talking with well-known saints of God, both those from the Bible and church history.
- Meeting and talking with saints of God we've never known, and hearing their stories of grace.
- Discovering all the joys God has prepared for us that we now know nothing about (1 Cor. 2:9). What are all these things God has prepared for those who love Him? I am eager to find out.

I remember the great delight and joy I felt as a three-year-old when I caught the first glimpse of Mother's car coming over the crest of that hill in the far distance. She was coming home, and I would be reunited with her! And what joy will fill our hearts when we get our first glimpse of our Lord and Savior, Jesus Christ. Whether that first glimpse comes when we enter His presence at death or when He returns to earth really doesn't matter. We will be forever in the presence of the One who loves us and gave Himself for us.

But this glorious future is only for those who belong to Christ. Those who have not repented of their sins and trusted Christ as their Lord and Savior have a future awaiting them as well—but it is not one to be eagerly anticipated. Rather it is a future to be greatly dreaded and feared.

So be sure you are in the company of those who belong to Christ, so you can eagerly anticipate the unimaginably glorious future God has prepared for those who love Him.

-12-

From God's Word, the Bible...

Now Cain talked with Abel his brother; and it came to pass, when they were in the field, that Cain rose up against Abel his brother and killed him.

Genesis 4:8

The Bible's Tragic Figures: Cain

The book of Genesis is the book of firsts. Adam was the first man. Eve was the first woman. Cain was the first son. Cain and Abel were the first brothers. Abel was the first man to die physically (there are other kinds of deaths). And Cain was the first hater and the first murderer. The reason Abel died is because Cain hated him and killed him.

In addition to his other "firsts," Cain was the man who engineered the first religious split. We have in Cain the beginning of a false religion. By the way, that religion is still alive and well. It is the religion of all those who believe that salvation comes to us by doing good works and not by depending completely on what God has provided in Christ.

Genesis 4 tells us that both Cain and Abel brought sacrifices to the Lord (v. 3), but the Lord wasn't pleased with Cain's. What was the difference between the two? The author of Hebrew informs us that Abel offered his sacrifice by faith or in faith, and Cain didn't (Heb. 11:4).

Faith made the difference! But what is faith? It's not, as so many seem to assume, mere positive thinking or optimism. Faith in the Bible is always believing in a message that God has revealed. The Apostle Paul writes: "So then faith comes by hearing, and hearing by the word of God" (Rom. 10:17).

We can't understand Cain and Abel if we don't go back to Genesis 3. There we have Adam and Eve falling into sin and God promising to send the Redeemer (Gen. 3:15). After making that promise, God made coverings for Adam and Eve by slaying animals (Gen. 3:21). That act was designed to show Adam and Eve something of what the Redeemer would do when He arrived on the scene. Those animals were innocent of Adam and Eve's sin, but God put them to death to cover Adam and Eve. In doing that, God was declaring that they could be fit to stand in His presence only on the basis of a substitute dying in their place. That's what the Redeemer would do. He would die as the substitute for sinners. The blood that He would shed would represent Him taking their place and receiving the penalty they deserved.

God has always had only one plan of salvation, and that plan is His Son. Sinners in the Old Testament were saved as they looked forward in faith to Christ. Sinners today are saved as they look backward in faith to Christ.

I don't hesitate to say that Adam and Eve were forgiven there in the Garden of Eden because they believed in the Redeemer that God had promised to send. They received a message from God, and they believed it. That's faith. And don't you know they also passed that message along to their sons? They would have wanted to be sure that their sons knew that they, too, must be forgiven by looking forward to the coming Christ.

Abel heard that message, believed it, and demonstrated his belief by shedding the blood of an animal just as God Himself had done in the garden of Eden. Cain, on the other hand, heard the same message. But he refused to accept it. He brought as his sacrifice some of the vegetables that he had grown. He came to God offering the work of his own hands.

We don't know how God made it clear to Cain that his sacrifice wasn't acceptable, but we know that He did. And we also know that He extended to Cain the opportunity to bring the right sacrifice (v. 7). But Cain, filled with anger and fury, refused to do what God wanted. He hated God and his way of salvation so very much that he took it out on Abel. He couldn't kill God, so he did the next best thing by killing his own brother.

On the day that Cain and Abel offered their sacrifices, the human race was divided into two streams: those who believe in God's plan of salvation and those who don't.

The message of Cain and Abel is plain. There is a way of salvation. That way is God's Son shedding His blood on the cross for sinners. We can accept it to our eternal blessing, or we can reject it to our eternal ruin. The Bible warns us about "the way of Cain" (Jude 11). That way consists of rejecting God's way.

-13-

From God's Word, the Bible...

And Jacob gave Esau bread and stew of lentils; then he ate and drank, arose, and went his way. Thus Esau despised his birthright.

Genesis 25:34

The Bible's Tragic Figures: Esau

The Bible presents us with many tragic figures. One of those is Esau, the grandson of Abraham and Sarah and the son of Isaac and Rebekah.

Esau had a twin brother, Jacob. But Esau was born first. That gave him something of enormous value in those days—the birthright. Among other important things, that meant he would receive a double portion of his father's inheritance.

Jacob wanted that birthright! He was probably motivated by the material wealth that it would eventually bring him.

The day came when Jacob saw his opportunity. Esau was hunting game. Jacob knew he would be famished when he returned, and he also knew very well the type of man that Esau was—the type that lives for the moment. Jacob had read his brother correctly. Esau was indeed the kind of man that wanted whatever craving he had at the moment to be satisfied in that moment.

So, Jacob had a stew ready and waiting when Esau

returned. When Esau demanded some, Jacob proposed a straightforward swap—the stew for the birthright! And Esau, that man of the moment, agreed.

It seems that this deal had no actual bearing on the eventual possession of the birthright. We learn later that Isaac was still planning to bless Esau as the possessor of the birthright. That plan would cause Jacob and his mother to shift into overdrive to thwart it. But the swap of the stew for the birthright did accurately reflect the character and the priorities of Esau and Jacob.

Here is the tragedy of Esau: he was willing to trade that which was of great and lasting importance for that which was of small and temporary value. The birthright for the stew! The future for the present!

So what do we have here? Is it only an ancient story that we find to be slightly entertaining? There's much to it than that! The truth is that Esau's bad bargain is one that has been made again and again throughout history, and it's one that is being made with incredible frequency these days.

Like Esau, we all possess something of enormous value. The Bible tells us that we aren't mere physical beings. We aren't just bodies. We are bodies and souls. And the Bible warns us to not ignore our souls. It urges us to not live for our physical needs while we ignore our greatest need, that is, the need of our souls. Jesus stated it very plainly: "For what is a man profited if he gains the whole world, and loses his own soul? Or what will a man give in exchange for his soul?" (Matt. 16:26).

Jesus also said: "Do not labor for the food which perishes, but for the food which endures to everlasting life. . . ." (John 6:27).

Jesus made the same point in his parable of the rich fool (Luke 12:13-21). The man, a farmer, was so obsessed with his crops and his barns that he gave no thought to his soul. And what did God require of him? Was it his crops or his barns? Here is the answer: "But God said to him, 'You fool! This night your soul will be required of you; then whose will those things be which you have provided?'" (v. 20).

There is only one way to properly care for our souls, and that is by committing them or entrusting them to the Lord Jesus Christ. He is the Savior.

Take care of the body? Yes, by all means. Protect it, feed it, wash it, and exercise it. But don't forget the soul. It's not a matter of choosing between caring for the body or caring for the soul. We can and should care for both, and, again, the only way to care for the soul is by trusting in what the Lord Jesus Christ came to this earth to do.

If Esau could speak audibly to us from eternity, he would plead with us to not let the passions and appetites of the moment blind us to eternal realities. Those realities may seem dim and distant now, but they will eventually become real and present to all of us—sooner perhaps than we think.

-14-

From God's Word, the Bible...

Then all the elders of Israel gathered together and came to Samuel at Ramah, and said to him, "Look, you are old, and your sons do not walk in your ways. Now make us a king to judge us like all the nations."

1 Samuel 8:4-5

The Bible's Tragic Figures: The Elders of Israel

That wonderful man of God, Samuel, was old, and the times, well, they were "a-changing." Up to this point, God had given leadership to the nation of Israel by providing them with judges (see the book of Judges). In keeping with that tradition, Samuel had appointed his sons "judges over Israel" (v. 1). We should note that this appointment came from Samuel, not from God. Samuel's two sons were nothing at all like their godly father (v. 3).

So the elders of Israel decided the time had come to take action. They wanted to end the "judge" tradition by installing a king. In their view, the time was ripe for Israel to take her place as an equal among the other nations.

There is no mention of these elders having consulted God. Had they done so, things would have been different. Had they looked into the book of Deuteronomy, they would have discovered that God didn't want Israel to be like all the other nations. He had put Israel on a pedestal from which she would have to step down in order to be like everyone else (Deut. 7:6-8; 28:9-10).

If the elders had sought the Lord's will, they would have found that He didn't want Israel to have a king at this time. Deuteronomy 17:14-20 indicates that God would give Israel a king in due time, but that time hadn't yet arrived.

Samuel's obvious displeasure (v. 6) should have been enough to derail the elders' plan for a king. Listening to Samuel had always brought blessing to the nation, and failing to listen to him had always brought trouble. But these men were so infatuated with having a king that they ignored their history.

Always a man of prayer, Samuel took the request of the elders to the Lord (v. 6). And, surprisingly, the Lord told him to give them a king. They were about to learn that it's not always a blessing when the Lord gives us what we want.

In obedience to the Lord's command, Samuel laid before the elders what they could expect from their king (vv. 9-17). At that point, they were crying for a king, but they would end up crying out because of their king (v. 18).

The warning was of no avail as these people "refused to obey the voice of Samuel" (v. 19). Their response to his words was to become even more adamant. They began by saying: "Now make us a king" (v. 5) and "Give us a king" (v. 6). They ended by saying: "...we will have a king..." (v. 19).

Why must we consider these elders of Israel to be among the Bible's tragic figures? The answer is plain. Their tragedy lay in their wanting to keep up with the times when they should have concerned themselves with keeping up with the truth. They had God's truth—there was to be no king at this time—but they willingly turned away from it. The key phrase in this situation is "like all the nations" (vv. 5,20).

Israel got their king, Saul, and they got nothing but heartache. After Saul came David, who was the king that God was planning to send them in His time. Perhaps the lesson from this episode could be put in this way: Don't settle for Saul while you wait for David.

Believers today can give into the "king thing" just as much as the elders of Samuel's time. We do so every time we set aside the truth of God in order to help the church keep up with the times. The Bible contains a straightforward message about the guilt of our sin and the holy nature of God that requires Him to judge our sin. It also plainly proclaims the judgment that God has determined, that is, eternal separation from Himself.

The Bible also declares God's gracious provision of forgiveness for sinners. That provision is Christ's death on the cross. That death consisted of Him receiving the wrath of God in the place of sinners. All who repent of their sins and trust in what Jesus did on that cross realize this precious truth: if Jesus received the wrath of God on the cross, there is no wrath left for those who receive Him.

The question ever before us is whether we will embrace the truth that God has set before us or whether we, like the elders of Israel, will set it aside so we can be considered up to date.

-15-

From God's Word, the Bible...

And Samuel said to Saul, "You have done foolishly. You have not kept the commandment of the LORD your God, which He commanded you. For now the LORD would have established your kingdom over Israel forever. But now your kingdom shall not continue. The LORD has sought for Himself a man after His own heart, and the LORD has commanded him to be commander over His people, because you have not kept what the LORD commanded you."

1 Samuel 13:13-14

The Bible's Tragic Figures: King Saul

Something was different in Israel. She now had a king. But something wasn't different. The nation was still to be governed by God's Word.

As Samuel turned the reins of leadership over to Saul, he spoke these solemn words: "Only fear the LORD and serve Him in truth with all your heart; for consider what great things He has done for you. But if you still do wickedly, both you and your king will be swept away" (12:24-25).

The success of the nation lay in both its king and people recognizing that God was their real king. It was the job of their earthly king to make sure that the nation obeyed the word of their heavenly king. If the Word of God was heard and obeyed, all would go well with the people and their king. But if they spurned God's Word, they would experience calamity. It was as simple as that.

Shortly after anointing Saul as king, Samuel made it clear to him that he would be tested on this matter of obeying

God's Word. The test would come in this form—before going into battle against the Philistines, Saul would have to wait at Gilgal for seven days until Samuel came to offer a sacrifice to the Lord and to show him, Saul, what he was to do.

How was Saul to know that Samuel was telling him the truth? The very day that he warned Saul about the upcoming test, he, Samuel, gave him three detailed prophecies. Each of those prophecies came true that very day (10:1-13)! Even more confirmations would come to Saul. One was his formal selection as king by the casting of lots. That random act would seem to make it far from certain that Saul would be chosen. But the lots were cast, and his tribe was chosen, then his family, and then him (10:20-21).

Yet another confirmation was when the Lord honored Samuel's word by causing it to thunder and rain when it never thundered and rained (12:16-18).

All of these things should have made Saul say to himself: "This man Samuel speaks the Word of God which is powerful and true, and when my day of testing comes, I'm going to do as Samuel has commanded."

Saul almost made it. Six days came and went, and he waited just as Samuel had commanded. The seventh day finally dawned, the day Samuel was supposed to arrive. The hours began to tick away, and there was no Samuel. Morning came and went, as did the afternoon, and Samuel was nowhere to be seen.

Saul convinced himself that he had to act. The Philistines were gathering all around, and his people, the Israelites, were scattering. It was true that the day wasn't over, but it seemed to Saul that Samuel had failed. So instead of waiting longer, Saul offered the sacrifice. He had just finished when Samuel came strolling down the path!

Saul had failed the test. He had been told to trust God's Word, but he caved in to the pressure of the moment. Saul was called to tremble at the thought of disobeying God's Word, but he chose instead to tremble at the mustering Philistines and scattering Israelites. Because he refused to take his stand on the Word of God, Saul couldn't rightly govern the people who were called to live on the basis of that Word. So Saul's reign over Israel was doomed to fail shortly after it started.

Modern Philistines ridicule the Bible and the gospel that it presents. They ridicule the preaching of Jesus' death on the cross as the only way of salvation. We can't expect Philistines to be other than what they are. But neither should we be intimidated by them. We must not pull the plug on the doctrines of Scripture merely because the modern Philistines reject them. The fact that Philistines are gathering doesn't mean that believers in Christ should scatter.

When we find ourselves being afraid that our preaching and sharing of the gospel will make us laughingstocks, we are trembling before the Philistines.

Each child of God either trembles before this intimidating world or before God's Word (Isa. 66:2). And, like Saul, we must each decide which we will do. Saul made the wrong decision and trembled before the wrong thing. With the Lord's help, we must make the right decision.

-16-

From God's Word, the Bible...

Then Amaziah said to Amos:
"Go, you seer!
Flee to the land of Judah.
There eat bread,
And there prophesy.
But never again prophesy at Bethel,
For it is the king's sanctuary,
And it is the royal residence."

Amos 7:12-13

The Bible's Tragic Figures: Amaziah

While Amaziah is not on the list of commonly known Bible characters, we need to know him. He is a tragic figure who emerges from the prophecy of Amos to urge us not to follow in his footsteps. What is the tragedy of Amaziah? It is that of attributing to mere men something that has come from God.

Amaziah is introduced to us as "the priest of Bethel" (v. 10). We might take that phrase to mean that he was a priest of the Lord. Amaziah was far from that. Bethel was the place where a former king of Israel, Jeroboam, had set up a false religion, one that was centered on the worship of a golden calf (1 Kings 12:28-29).

Now another Jeroboam was on the throne of Israel, and the idolatrous worship of the calf continued unabated at Bethel.

Everything seemed to be going splendidly in Israel. It was a time of prosperity and stability (Amos 3:12,15; 4:1; 6:4,6), and religion was flourishing (4:4; 5:5,21-23; 8:3,10). A nice, comfortable complacency had settled over the land.

One day Amos, a true prophet of the Lord, showed up to shatter the complacency. He declared that God was opposed to their idolatry and would shatter the idolatrous worship of Bethel (3:13-15). He also declared that the people of Israel would be carried into captivity by a foreign nation (5:2; 6:7). Amos' message was about God's wrath against sin and about judgment to come.

Amaziah was so agitated by this message that he first reported Amos to the king (7:10-11) and then confronted Amos himself (7:12-13). It's easy to see Amaziah's assumption, namely, Amos' message wasn't to be explained in terms of coming from God but rather in terms of Amos' own thinking. As far as Amaziah was concerned, Amos' message wasn't divine. It was nothing more than a mere man offering his own assessment. Since Amos' message was a mere human message, Amos could take it elsewhere. So Amaziah told the prophet to prophesy in the land of Judah but never again at Bethel (7:12-13a).

The one thing that never occurred to Amaziah was the possibility that Amos was not at Bethel by his own choice. He was there because God had sent him. And Amos' message was not his own invention. It was rather God's revelation.

Amos was quick to set Amaziah straight on these matters. He affirmed that it was God who "took" him while he was following his sheep, and it was God who plainly said to him: "Go, prophesy to My people Israel" (7:15).

This exchange between Amaziah and Amos was not merely a matter of charge and countercharge. Amos had evidence on his side. He could point to the Law of Moses that clearly declared that God would judge the idolatry of His people (Deut. 4:26-28; 6:13-15; 8:19-20; 30:17-18). Furthermore, he could point to instances in which God had visited their forefathers with judgment for going after idols, one of which was judgment for the worship of a golden calf (Ex. 32:1-6,27-28). Still further, Amos could point to things in Israel that indicated that God was already bringing the good times to an end (4:6-11).

But the evidence meant nothing to Amaziah. He was so much in love with his own world that he couldn't accept Amos' message. He looked at Bethel and saw there the king's sanctuary and his residence. It was all so marvelous, and he, Amaziah, was part of it all! He allowed it to blind him to the divine character of Amos' message, to the judgment to come on Israel, and to his own judgment (7:17).

We are confronted in the Bible with a message that claims to be from God. It's a message about our sin and about eternal judgment to come. It's also a message about the way that we can have our sins forgiven and escape coming judgment. That way is Jesus. On the basis of His perfect life and substitutionary death on the cross, guilty sinners can stand acceptably in God's presence.

Although this message is backed by abundant evidence, many dismiss it as Amaziah dismissed Amos' message. They see it as a message that men have invented. They ignore the lesson that tragic Amaziah teaches—to treat a divine message as less than divine doesn't destroy it, but rather it destroys those who reject it.

-17-

From God's Word, the Bible...

Then Judas, His betrayer, seeing that He had been condemned, was remorseful and brought back the thirty pieces of silver to the chief priests and elders, saying,
"I have sinned by betraying innocent blood."
And they said, "What is that to us? You see to it!"

Matthew 27:3-4

The Bible's Tragic Figures: Judas

There was actually a man who preached his own funeral service. When the time for the service came, one of his sons walked up to the pulpit and activated the playback button on a recording device. And the people heard the voice of the dearly departed. Those who knew their Bibles probably thought of that phrase in Hebrews 11:4: "he being dead yet speaks."

Judas Iscariot has been dead for many centuries, but he is also still speaking. You remember Judas. He is one of the most tragic figures in all of history. What a stained name is his! Chosen as one of Jesus' original twelve disciples, Judas turned against the Lord. For thirty pieces of silver, he arranged to have Jesus arrested. A few hours after his treacherous act, Judas threw those pieces of silver at the feet of those who had paid him and went out to hang himself.

The religious authorities, who weren't scrupulous at all about arresting, trying, and executing Jesus, were very scrupulous about the money Judas returned. It must not go into the temple treasury! That would be sacrilege! So they used it to buy a field to bury strangers in. Becoming known as "Field of Blood," it was evidently the place in which Judas killed himself.

We have the account of Judas in the Bible so we can hear that tragic man speak to us. And what does the long-dead Judas have to say? The first thing is this: *the fact that we enjoy marvelous spiritual privileges doesn't mean we have been truly saved*.

No one ever enjoyed more spiritual privileges than Judas. Jesus, the greatest of all preachers, preached the greatest of all sermons, and Judas was there to hear them. Jesus performed many miracles and all kinds of miracles, and Judas was there to see them. But with it all, Judas was an unsaved man (John 6:70-71).

We can also enjoy many spiritual privileges and still be lost. We can attend many church services, hear many sermons, read many wonderful books about the things of God, and yet never come to a true and living faith in Christ. Let us beware!

Judas also tells us that *it is crucial to accept the Lord Jesus for what He is and not for what we want Him to be*.

Have you ever wondered why Judas betrayed Jesus? The answer is bound up in the kind of kingdom that Judas was interested in. Judas wanted Jesus to set up an earthly kingdom. He, Judas, was a man of the here and now. After following Jesus for three years or so, it became apparent to him that Jesus wasn't going to do that. Some suggest that Judas decided to betray Jesus in order to force His hand. If Jesus were placed in the position of facing death, He would then use His power to defeat His enemies and establish the kingdom that Judas wanted Him to establish.

Yes, Jesus had come to this earth to set up a kingdom, but His kingdom was not to be of this earth. While Judas was out hanging himself, Jesus was speaking these words to Pontius Pilate: "My kingdom is not of this world. If my kingdom were of this world, My servants would fight, so that I should not be delivered to the Jews; but now My kingdom is not from here" (John 18:36).

The kingdom of Christ is spiritual in nature. It is set up in the hearts of sinners when the grace of God stirs them to repentance and brings them to faith in Christ. While King Jesus is now setting up His kingdom in the hearts of His people, there will come a day in which His rule will be open and obvious. On that day, every knee will bow before Him, and every tongue will confess that He is the King of Kings and the Lord of Lords (Phil. 2:9-11; Rev. 19:16).

But many, like Judas, aren't interested in that kind of kingdom. They would rather have a Christ who helps them in this world instead of preparing them to enter the next world. Meanwhile, they fail to see that nothing helps us more in this life than the confidence that we are ready for the life to come.

The still-speaking Judas urges us not to repeat his thinking and his doing. Are we willing to listen to him?

-18-

From God's Word, the Bible...

"To whom then will you liken Me,
Or to whom shall I be equal?" says the Holy One.

For thus says the LORD,
Who created the heavens,
Who is God,
Who formed the earth and made it,
Who has established it,
Who did not create it in vain,
Who formed it to be inhabited:
"I am the LORD, and there is no other."

Isaiah 40:25; 45:18

The Hymn of the Three C's

What are the most treasured and well-liked of all the hymns? Every list I have seen includes *How Great Thou Art*. Others, as you might suppose, are *Amazing Grace*, *The Old Rugged Cross*, *Holy, Holy, Holy* and *Blessed Assurance*.

How Great Thou Art came to us down a winding road. It went from Sweden to Germany to Russia before coming to the United Kingdom and America.

It was written by Carl Gustav Boberg in Monsteras, Sweden, in 1885. One Sunday afternoon, twenty-six-year-old Boberg was making his way home from the church that he served as pastor when he was caught in a terrific thunderstorm. After finding shelter, Boberg marveled at the power of the storm. When it passed, Boberg took notice of the beautiful rainbow and the happy singing of the birds. It all made such a profound impression on him that he took up his pen and poured out adoration and worship to God. The hymn was eventually translated from Russian to English by missionary

Stuart Hine in 1949. It was greatly popularized by George Beverly Shea and Cliff Barrows in the Billy Graham crusades.

It's the hymn of the Three "C's," taking us from creation to the cross to the culmination of all things. The marvel of God's creation is set forth in the first two verses:

> *O Lord my God! When I in awesome wonder*
> *Consider all the works Thy hand hath made.*
> *I see the stars, I hear the rolling thunder,*
> *Thy power throughout the universe displayed.*
>
> *When through the woods and forest glades I wander*
> *And hear the birds sing sweetly in the trees;*
> *When I look down from lofty mountain grandeur*
> *And hear the brook and feel the gentle breeze.*

With these things in place, the refrain is inevitable. It is a burst of triumphant praise:

> *Then sings my soul, my Savior God, to Thee:*
> *How great Thou art, how great Thou art!*
> *Then sings my soul, my Savior God, to Thee:*
> *How great Thou art, how great Thou art!*

The hymn takes us to the cross in these moving words:

> *And when I think that God, His Son not sparing,*
> *Sent Him to die, I scarce can take it in;*
> *That on the cross, my burden gladly bearing,*
> *He bled and died to take away my sin.*

That verse, of course, also calls for the same triumphant burst of praise in the refrain as the verses about God's creative wonders. Does the cross of Christ fill us with adoring wonder? If it doesn't we should ponder deeply the gap between our "burden" and the "gladly bearing." Our burden was our sin that justly deserved the wrath of God. On the cross, Jesus not only took that burden, but also took it willingly and gladly. Can it be? Jesus gladly took the burden of my sin and judgment so I don't have to carry that burden any longer! Let me realize this to the point that I can sing, "Then sings my soul. . . ."

Then there's that great verse of culmination:

When Christ shall come with shout of acclamation
And take me home, what joy shall fill my heart!
Then I shall bow in humble adoration,
And there proclaim, my God, how great Thou art!

That verse also leads quite inevitably to the refrain. Perhaps there has never been a more happy marriage between verses and refrain than the one we find in this superb hymn.

In my estimation, the church needs to sing this hymn and sing it often. The reason is that she, the church, is starved for a sense of the greatness of God. The problem isn't that God is withholding the evidences of His greatness from us. It's rather that we are depriving ourselves of His greatness by our fascination with little things. Pastors and church-goers seem to take enormous delight in the troubleshooter God who concerns Himself with helping us cope with the aggravations, frustrations, and irritations that crop up in daily living. Our need is to lift our eyes from our little living to see the wonders of the creation, the cross, and the culmination until we join Boberg in boisterously singing to the Lord: "How great Thou art!"

-19-

From God's Word, the Bible...

O God, You have taught me from my youth;
And to this day I declare Your wondrous works.
Now also when I am old and grayheaded,
O God, do not forsake me,
Until I declare Your strength to this generation,
Your power to everyone who is to come.

Psalm 71:17-18

An Old Man with a Flat Tire

I don't think of myself as old, but I sometimes get reminded in a jolting sort of way that I am. Sylvia and I were returning from a church service one night when our car warned us that we were losing air in one of our rear tires. We pulled into a convenience store parking lot to take a look. The problem was easy to see. A steel rod had gone through one side of the tire and had come out the other side. The tire was now completely flat.

I immediately ran into a problem. There was a lever that had to be pulled to release the spare tire, but it was tucked so neatly away that I was having a hard time locating it. The woman who was working in the convenience store came to my rescue. She knew a man inside the store who would be willing to help. Out he came, and in mere minutes had the tire changed.

It was when I offered to pay him something for helping that I received my jolt. He refused with these words: "I never take money from an old man that needs help."

Then and there I knew—in blunt and brutal fashion—I am an old man. These words from David quickly sprang to my mind:

> *I have been young, and now am old. . . .*
> (Ps. 37:25a)

I find as I advance in years that I can relate very easily to the picture of old age in the opening verses of Ecclesiastes 12:

- the keepers of the house tremble;
- the strong men bow down;
- the grinders cease because they are few;
- those that look through the windows grow dim;
- the doors are shut in the streets;
- the daughters of music are brought low;
- the almond tree blossoms.

These descriptive phrases relate to the hands, the legs, the teeth, the eyes, the ears, the voice, and the hair (which turns white, or in my case, loose). I can especially identify with this part of old age—"one rises up at the sound of a bird." That is the author's way of depicting the old person being easily awakened from sleep. I know what it is to wake up at the sound of a bird—and it doesn't have to be a very big bird.

Ecclesiastes 12:5 humorously adds another detail of old age: "The grasshopper is a burden." If a grasshopper should land on the shoulder of an old person, it would seem to be a heavy load. The same verse also tells us that "desire fails," that is, the old person isn't interested in doing things that used to fire his interest.

This passage is depressing if we forget to lay the blessings of old age alongside the burdens. And old age does have its blessings. I try to keep in mind that I could have died at a very young age (I had a couple of close calls) and been deprived of many years of happiness and satisfaction.

As the years slide by—ever more rapidly it seems—I also try to remind myself to look forward to heaven. We Christians are supposed to know that this world isn't our home. We are pilgrims who are traveling through this world to our true home in heaven. But if we're not careful we can get so attached to this world that we're not looking forward to heaven. Matthew Henry cautions us that the world is a traveling place, not a stopping place. We need that caution.

I would like to see more yearning for heaven. In my years as a pastor I detected an attitude among many believers that could be put like this: "If I have to leave this world, I guess heaven is better than the other place."

Heaven will not just be better than "the other place." It's going to be great! Let's keep reminding ourselves of that and coach ourselves to look forward to it.

I also want to use my older years to be ever more grateful to the Lord Jesus for His redeeming work on my behalf. He is my way to heaven.

I'm grateful to the man who changed my tire. I'm also grateful that he called me an old man. It made me think about old age, and I realized that it's not bad to be old.

-20-

From God's Word, the Bible...

But someone will say, "How are the dead raised up?
And with what body do they come?"

1 Corinthians 15:35

Dr. Brown's Body

I was the guest preacher. The Sunday evening worship service began with the congregation singing a hymn. After that a gentleman came to the pulpit to share this announcement: "It is my sad responsibility to inform you that Dr. Brown passed away this afternoon."

Dr. Brown had been retired for a long time after being the pastor of that church for close to thirty years. He had served with distinction and was widely and highly esteemed.

Since Dr. Brown had been ill for quite some time, I wasn't surprised to hear that he had died. I was surprised to hear the next words from the man who was making the announcement. He said: "Dr. Brown has already received that new body that the Bible promises."

The Christian will definitely receive a new body. There should be no doubt about that. But the Christian doesn't receive his new body when he dies. That comes later.

When the believer dies, a separation takes place. The soul is separated from the body, and the soul goes immediately into the presence of God. The Apostle Paul describes the believer's death as being "absent from the body" and being "present with the Lord" (2 Cor. 5:8). It's certainly correct to say that a believer goes to heaven when he dies, but that is true of the soul only.

What happens to the body of the believer? Generally speaking, it goes into the grave. So, when the believer dies his soul goes to heaven and his body goes to the grave.

Is that the final word for the body? No, not at all! The body will eventually be raised from the grave and will be reunited with the soul. But that won't happen until Jesus comes again. That's when Dr. Brown will get his new body, but not until then.

The souls of dead believers are at perfect peace with the Lord, but they also yearn for that day when they will be reunited with their bodies. We might say they are now happy but incomplete. Their condition could be pictured in terms of a young couple who are engaged to be married. They are happy during their engagement, but they aren't complete. And they eagerly look forward to their wedding day when they will be complete.

The resurrection of the body and the reunion of it with the soul is "the blessed hope" of the Christian (Titus 2:13). Then the Christian will be complete.

After hearing me preach on the resurrection of the Christian's body, a lady angrily confronted me after the service with this question: "Why would we want these old bodies back?"

She was assuming that the resurrection of the body means getting this body back as it is now. It was evident that she had not read with understanding the teaching of Paul in 1 Corinthians 15. The Apostle says there's a sense in which Christians will get their bodies back. Those bodies that go into the graves will come out of the graves. But the bodies that come out of those graves will surpass those that go into it, just as plants that spring from the ground far surpass the seeds that go into the ground.

Paul informs us that these bodies are "sown in corruption," that is, they are subject to decay and deterioration, but the bodies that are raised from the graves will be "incorruptible" (v. 42). Further, these bodies are "sown in dishonor" (v. 3). There is no dignity or honor in death! But when Jesus comes to raise His people, the dishonor will be gone as our new bodies are clothed in glory. Still further, Paul tells us that these bodies are "natural" (v. 44). They were made for this natural realm and are suited for it, but when Jesus comes, they will be raised and suited to the eternal world.

While we don't have all the answers that we might desire about the nature of the resurrected bodies of believers, it should be enough for us to know that those bodies will be modeled and fashioned after the resurrection body the Lord Jesus has (vv. 45-49; 1 John 3:2).

It was my privilege to know Dr. Brown. He was a good and godly man. His soul is now with the Lord, and his body is in the grave. If his body lying there in the grave could hear, I would say: "Wait a little longer. Glory is coming!"

-21-

From God's Word, the Bible...

If we confess our sins, He is faithful and just to forgive us our sins and to cleanse us from all unrighteousness.

1 John 1:9

Pushing the Pool or Moving the Bucket

Our grandchildren were playing in one of those inflatable pools. You know the kind. Fill it with air and put water in it, and, presto, you have a swimming pool. It took a lot of water to fill this pool, so much so that it was very heavy and impossible to move around.

The children also had water guns that could shoot a stream of water for an impressive distance. One of their favorite games was to sit in the pool with those guns while they tried to shoot water into a bucket a few feet from the pool. But there was a problem. They had stationed the bucket so far away that they were having trouble hitting it. Our grandson, Isaiah, came up with a solution. He asked his dad to move the pool closer to the bucket!

It occurred to me that I have often been guilty of trying to do the very thing that Isaiah suggested, that is, to move the pool when it would have been much easier to move the bucket.

The Christian life is hard. The Bible never hides that fact. It likens it to carrying a cross (Matt. 16:24). That's hard. It also pictures the Christian as a soldier in a war, an athlete competing in a race, and a farmer trying to raise a crop (2 Tim. 2:3-6). Each of those professions requires diligent, devoted effort, and each involves danger of some kind. Those who suggest that there is a formula for taking the difficulty out of Christian living simply don't know what they're talking about.

Because Christian living is so difficult in and of itself, the very last thing we need to do is to make it more difficult. The difficulty that the Lord has put in it should be enough for us without adding difficulties of our own. That's what the devil would like for us to do. He wants us to rise from our beds each morning and start shoving on a very heavy pool instead of moving the bucket.

What pool does the devil have you shoving around? Is it guilt? That's an impossibly heavy pool to shove around!

King David knew about guilt. He had done terrible things, committing adultery with Bathsheba, having her husband murdered, and then trying to cover it all up. For a long time, he lived with horrible guilt. He speaks of "groaning all the day long" (Ps. 32:3).

Here in David's own words is how he found relief:

> *I acknowledged my sin to You,*
> *And my iniquity I have not hidden,*
> *I said, "I will confess my transgressions to the LORD,"*
> *And You forgave the iniquity of my sin.*
> (Ps. 32:5)

David's relief came when he repented of his sins, and he is quick to assure us that all of God's people can find relief from their guilt in the same way:

For this cause everyone who is godly shall pray to You. . . .
(Ps. 32:6a)

Repentance is turning from our sins to God. To turn toward something, we have to turn away from something. To turn toward God, we have turn away from sin. We have to do an about face. Before we repent, our faces are toward sin and our backs toward God. When we repent we turn our backs toward our sins and our faces toward God.

If we're living with the heaviness of guilt, we must repent! The Lord gives marvelous assurances to all who sincerely repent. In regard to sins of which we repent, the Lord promises:

- to remove them from us as far as the east is from the west (Ps. 103:12);
- to pass over them (Micah 6:18);
- to cast them into the depths of the sea (Micah 7:19);
- to put them behind His back (Isa. 38:17);
- to blot them out (Isa 44:22);
- to remember them no more (Jer. 31:34);
- to make them impossible to find (Jer. 50:20).

Repentance itself is not an easy thing. We must have grace from God to do it. Let's ask God for that grace, and let's always remember that repentance is much less difficult than living daily with crushing guilt. The yoke of Christ is light compared to that of sin (Matt. 11:28-30). We might say that repentance, as difficult as it is, is like moving a bucket. Living with guilt is like trying to push a pool. So let's move the bucket.

-22-

From God's Word, the Bible...

For you know the grace of our Lord Jesus Christ, that though He was rich, yet for your sakes He became poor, that you through His poverty might become rich.

2 Corinthians 8:9

From Riches to Poverty to Riches

A Reading from Sylvia

In the mid to late 1940s, my mother and I were living with my widowed grandmother. My mother was also a widow, my father having been killed in World War II before I was born. Mother was a career woman with a good job that she enjoyed. She wore nice clothes and shoes. My grandmother's house was nicer than most homes in our small community. Mother had paid to have a bathroom installed, which was a luxury few homes in our community had. Grandma took care of me while Mother was at work. So life was good, comfortable, and quite easygoing for Mother.

And then she met Gene Miller, a poor, struggling farmer. After a brief courtship they were married, and Mother's life drastically changed. She quit her job, and we moved to a farm seventeen miles from town. My new dad didn't own the farm; he just rented the land and the small four-room house that came with it.

The house had no electricity, no running water, and, of course, no bathroom. It was located two miles from the highway, and before the road reached our house it changed from a gravel road to a dirt road. That meant when it rained, the dirt road became a mud road and sometimes so impassable that we had to leave our car at the end of the gravel road and walk through the mud the last quarter of a mile to our house.

Why did my mother give up the easy life she had in exchange for a difficult life as the wife of a poor farmer? It was love. She loved Dad enough to become poor with him.

The Lord Jesus Christ did a similar thing for us, but on a much greater scale. He left the beauty, glory, and riches of heaven to come to this earth in our humanity. His life of perfect obedience to the Father was marked by poverty and difficulty (Matt. 8:20). Then He died on the cross a death like no one else has ever died, taking upon Himself our sins and receiving the full fury of God's wrath against those sins.

And why did He do it? It was love. He loved us enough to lay aside the riches He enjoyed in heaven and become poor, so that we who were poor in our sins and hopelessness could become rich. No, this isn't referring to monetary riches, but to the greater riches that are ours as believers in Christ: forgiveness of sins, right standing with God, and an eternal home in heaven.

What was the result of Christ's willingness to come to this earth to carry out the plan of redemption? A multitude of people who were poor in their sins and living under the judgment of God have become rich.

And what were the results of my mother's willingness to marry Gene Miller? After a few months we got electricity in that little house and a pump at the kitchen sink to bring in cold water. Four years later, Mom and Dad were able to purchase a farm of their own closer to town. It had a large farmhouse that Dad turned into a comfortable home where Mom lived until her death. As a result of the choice Mom made, she and I both became rich. No, not monetarily, but in much better ways. Mother acquired a husband who loved her devotedly the rest of her life. I acquired a wonderful Christian father who couldn't have loved me more if I had been his own flesh and blood. God blessed their marriage with four sons who adored their mom, and my life was enriched by growing up with siblings.

I am so thankful that Mother chose to lay aside her comfortable life and financial stability to become poor for a season so that she and I could become rich in many ways. And oh, how much more thankful I am that the Lord Jesus Christ chose to lay aside His riches and become poor for a season to enrich me with His glorious salvation.

-23-

From God's Word, the Bible...

Blessed is he whose transgression is forgiven,
Whose sin is covered.

Psalm 32:1

Simple Song, Sublime Truth

Too great a sinner to be saved! That's what Walter "Happy Mac" MacDonald thought many years ago. Although he had built a reputation for himself as a dancer, his sinful living had made him miserable. One evening in the early 1930s he made his way into a meeting of the Pacific Garden Mission in Chicago and heard the gospel. Although the workers there urged him to turn to Christ, he refused. But he kept attending the services.

Walter and Ethelwyn Taylor, known as Pa and Ma Taylor, were leading this mission effort. Ma Taylor carried a special burden for Happy Mac and prayed for his salvation. When he finally came for counseling, he poured out to the Lord these sorrowful words: "You don't know how bad I am, Lord. Really, I'm the worst man in the world. You can't save me; I'm too bad."

Upon hearing that prayer, Ma Taylor recalled some words she had recently heard from a preacher. This preacher, Percy

Crawford, had been a very sinful young man, but he turned to the Lord. In relating his conversion, Crawford said: "Calvary covers it all." Ma shared those words with Happy Mac, who immediately embraced them and trusted Christ.

Soon after that Ma Taylor wrote these words:

> *Far dearer than all that the world can impart*
> *Was the message that came to my heart;*
> *How that Jesus alone*
> *For my sin did atone,*
> *And Calvary covers it all.*

> Chorus:
> *Calvary covers it all,*
> *My past with its sin and stain;*
> *My guilt and despair*
> *Jesus took on Him there,*
> *And Calvary covers it all.*

This is a simple song, consisting of short, plain words, the longest of which has ten letters. That word is "redemption," which appears in this verse:

> *How matchless the grace, when I looked on the face*
> *Of this Jesus, my crucified Lord;*
> *My redemption complete*
> *I then found at His feet,*
> *And Calvary covers it all.*

Here is the sublime truth of Ma Taylor's simple hymn: Calvary covers it all! Are you a big sinner? Jesus is a bigger Savior than you are a sinner!

What is sin? It is refusing to live the way that God requires. God has given us certain commandments by which He expects us to live. Look at the Ten Commandments in Exodus 20:1-17. Each one of those commandments testifies against us. Not one of us has perfectly kept them, and each broken commandment shouts the word "Sinner" at us.

The problem with being sinners is that we eventually have to come before the God who gave these commandments. If we stand before Him in our sins, He will drive us from His presence into everlasting ruin. But if those sins are covered, hidden from His view, He will receive us.

Jesus' death on the cross provides the covering we need. He received the penalty for sinners so all who trust in Him will not receive that penalty themselves. Because of what Jesus did on the cross, God throws a cover over our sins so He can no longer see them. Sin covered so that it can no longer be seen—what a blessed thought! And it's Jesus' death on the cross of Calvary that provides the cover.

The Ark of the Covenant in the Old Testament pictures this. The Ten Commandments were placed in the lower part of the Ark. Above those commandments was the Mercy Seat where the High Priest sprinkled the blood of the sacrifice. The Mercy Seat was exactly the same width as the box that contained the commandments. The Ark, then, gave this testimony: the blood of the atonement was sufficient to cover the broken commandments.

Those who trust Christ, no matter how sinful they have been, are saved and can now sing:

> *How blessed the thought, that my soul by Him bought,*
> *Shall be His in the glory on high;*
> *Where with gladness and song*
> *I'll be one of the throng,*
> *And Calvary covers it all.*

-24-

From God's Word, the Bible...

*Therefore, whether you eat or drink, or whatever you do,
do all to the glory of God.*

1 Corinthians 10:31

I Am Resolved

Determination, not desire, is the key to spiritual attainment. Many of us desire to progress in spirituality. The problem is that we're not determined to progress.

A great example of determination is Jonathan Edwards. Before he was twenty years of age, he wrote seventy resolutions to guide and govern his spiritual life. These resolutions can easily be found online.

We often assume that we can't expect young people to be concerned about growing in grace and in the knowledge of the Lord. We tend to think God has a cheaper, easier brand of Christianity for them and doesn't expect much out of them until they are adults.

Edwards thought differently. If one's youthful years aren't too early to be saved by Christ from eternal woe, they surely aren't too early to give to the Lord a heart of love and to plan for a life of devotion. If one is saved from a very serious situation, such a person should be very serious about the Lord.

Edwards' resolutions throb with a seriousness that puts most of us to shame. Ours seems to be a time in which it's never possible to be too lighthearted and casual about Christianity, but it's always possible to be too serious about it.

Edwards' resolutions suggest to me a threefold division—the preeminent, the prominent and the prudent.

With the word *preeminent*, I'm referring to the priority of his life, which was living for the glory of God. It's very significant that the first resolution begins: "I will do whatsoever I think to be most to the glory of God...."

What is it to live for the glory of God? It's to live in such a way that the credit for our lives goes to God. It's to live in such a way that others will have to note that there are higher principles at work, and that those principles come, not from within ourselves, but from God.

Many regard this kind of living as detrimental to happiness. Edwards didn't. In his first resolution, he inserts the words "my own good, profit, and pleasure" immediately after "the glory of God." As far as he was concerned, the two were one and the same—living for God's glory and experiencing happiness. Holiness doesn't destroy our happiness; it secures it. Edwards wanted to be happy here, but he also wanted to live in such a way as to obtain "much happiness in the other world" (Resolution #22).

With the word *prominent*, I'm referring to those realities of which he was always conscious—realities that drove him to make God his priority.

Death is one of those realities. Edwards often reminds himself to live with death in mind. In one resolution, he reminds himself to "think much, on all occasions, of my dying." The awareness of death, of course, should bring with it the awareness of our accountability to God for how we have lived. With Edwards, death and judgment were inseparably linked.

Edwards' also lived with the ongoing awareness of how very inclined we are to sin and how very necessary it is for us to concern ourselves with "the state" of our souls. Resolution

#48 reads: "Resolved, constantly, with the utmost niceness and diligence, and the strictest scrutiny, to be looking into the state of my soul, that I may know whether I have truly an interest in Christ or no; that when I come to die, I may not have any negligence respecting this to repent of."

If we want to achieve a higher level of spirituality, we would do well to think frequently, as Edwards did, about death, judgment, sin, and the state of our souls.

With the word *prudent*, I'm referring to the practical steps he took. We should note that his concern for holy living extended to every aspect of life, including usage of time, treatment of animals, assurance, prayer, faithfulness, speaking, the Lord's Day, eating and drinking, respect for parents, general attitudes, and afflictions.

All of Edwards' resolutions search me, but none more than these:

- "To strive every week to be brought higher in religion, and to a higher exercise of grace, than I was the week before" (#30);
- To never ". . .act as if I were any way my own, but entirely and altogether God's. . ." (#43);
- To live in such a way as to have "Christianity always shining in its true lustre" (#63).

Can we do as well as Edwards did? Probably not. Can we do better than we are doing? Yes. And the first step in doing better must surely be to think long and hard about what the Lord Jesus has done for us. In heaven's glory, He thought of us; God the Father and Jesus resolved that He would come into this world to live a perfect life and die a sacrificial death for sinners, and then rise again in justification of all who would trust Him. Such was His resolution for us; are we resolved to live for Him and His glory?

-25-

From God's Word, the Bible...

"Most assuredly, I say to you, he who hears My word and believes in Him who sent Me has everlasting life, and shall not come into judgment, but has passed from death into life."

John 5:24

The Voice of Christ

The words of our verse occur in the midst of a section that stresses the voice of Christ. The word "hear" appears four times in this section (vv. 24-29), while the word "voice" appears twice and "word" appears once.

Ours is a time of voices competing for our attention and allegiance. The voices of pleasure, possessions, politics, and position speak to us in alluring tones. The voice of Christ often seems to be drowned out by the other voices, but it is still sounding, and, like the others, it also calls for our allegiance.

Why should we give priority to hearing the voice of Christ? First, *it is the voice of absolute authority.*

The authority of Jesus is the central issue in John 5. The chapter begins with Jesus healing a man who had been lame for thirty-eight years (vv. 1-9). This would seem to have caused great rejoicing, but there was a fly in the ointment. Jesus healed this man on the Sabbath (v. 9). The religious leaders of the Jews were so incensed over Jesus doing this that they actually sought to kill Him (v. 16).

Jesus added fuel to the fire by claiming that this miracle was the result of Him and God the Father working together (v. 17). The religious leaders understood what Jesus was saying. He was claiming to be equal with God (v. 18). They were right.

Beginning in verse 19, Jesus defended His claim by saying three times "Most assuredly, I say to you. . ." (vv. 19,24,25). Jesus used this phrase when He wanted to call attention to something of tremendous importance. John's Gospel relates twelve such occasions.

These words are, in and of themselves, a claim of authority. When we want to establish our authority for saying something, we quote experts in that field. But there was no higher authority for Jesus to quote. So when He was dealing with something that required authority, He merely said: "I say to you."

We see Him doing this in the Sermon on the Mount. Several times He indicated what the religious leaders were teaching the people and then corrected each of those teachings with these words: "But I say to you" (Matt. 5:17-48). Those who heard Him noted His authority (Matt. 7:29).

We should understand that Jesus' authority was also substantiated by the witness of John the Baptist (vv. 31-35), by the miracles that He performed (v. 36), and by God the Father Himself (v. 37).

All of these evidences for Jesus converge in a mighty way to tell us that we should listen to His voice. It is the voice of authority.

A second reason for us to listen to the voice of Christ is this: *it is the voice that announces wonderful news.*

Jesus says: ". . . he who hears My word and believes in Him who sent Me has everlasting life. . ." (v. 24).

Wonderful news indeed! All who believe in Jesus have everlasting life! Jesus doesn't say: "he who is rich," or "he who is very intelligent," or "he who enjoys fame and status." No, He says, ". . . he who hears My voice and believes in Him who sent Me." That is the person who receives everlasting life.

Hearing and believing! How can we hear the word of Jesus? We can hear it by reading the Bible and by listening to the preaching and teaching of the Bible. That is where the Lord Jesus speaks. We must hear before we can believe. Paul writes: "So then faith comes by hearing, and hearing by the word of God" (Rom. 10:17).

What is it to believe? It's not just knowing the facts about the Lord Jesus and believing those facts to be true. It is a matter of committing ourselves to Him as the only possible way for our sins to be forgiven.

There's yet another reason we should pay close attention to the voice of Christ. *It is the voice that announces what happens to those who refuse to believe.* Those who refuse Christ "come into judgment" (v. 24).

Jesus is the bridge or the passageway from the land of condemnation into the land of life. Those who refuse to heed His voice and use Him as their bridge must remain in condemnation. To have life, we must have Jesus, and to have Jesus we must hear His voice and believe in Him (John 3:18,36; 14:6; 1 John 5:12).

Have you heard the voice of Jesus in His Word, the Bible, and are you trusting Him alone for your salvation?

.

-26-

From God's Word, the Bible...

And take the helmet of salvation, and the sword of the Spirit, which is the word of God; praying always with all prayer and supplication in the Spirit, being watchful to this end with all perseverance and supplication for all the saints —

Ephesians 6:17-18

The Word and Prayer

The church is engaged in spiritual warfare. This stems from her having an enemy—Satan. While he can roar like a lion (1 Peter 5:8), Satan often prefers to do his work by relying on his ability to deceive. He is so effective with this strategy that Paul repeatedly warns his readers to not be deceived (1 Cor. 3:18; 15:33; Gal. 6:7; Eph 5:6; 2 Thess. 2:3).

To fight Satan and his forces we must put on the armor of God. The following parts of the armor are defensive in nature: the girdle of truth (v. 14a), the breastplate of righteousness (v. 14b), the feet shod with the preparation of the gospel of peace (v. 15), the shield of faith (v. 16) and the helmet of salvation (v. 17a).

After listing those items, Paul proceeds to call attention to the weapon that Christians have been given, namely, "the sword of the Spirit which is the word of God" (Eph. 6:17b). The Word of God is for both defense and offense. By relying on its teachings, we can fend off Satan's attack. By wielding it in proclamation, we can put him and his forces to flight. The reason is the Word of God is a very powerful weapon (Heb. 4:12).

When the church as a whole employs this weapon, she will see Satan's strongholds or fortifications fall. And the arguments Satan plants in sinners, arguments that they use to exalt themselves against the knowledge of God, will be cast down. Through the power of the Word of God, the church can expect to see such sinners captured and brought into obedience of Christ (2 Cor. 10:4-5).

It is interesting that Paul wraps up his description of the Christian's armor by calling his readers to pray "always with all prayer and supplication in the Spirit" (v. 18).

Some have wondered why he didn't include prayer as part of the armor. The reason may very well be that he wanted to emphasize that each part of the armor is to be taken up and employed with prayer.

Prayer isn't to be the casual, nonchalant muttering of words. It must be sincere and fervent. We must not be casual about war! Warfare praying requires certain things. First, we are to use "all prayer," that is, every form of prayer. Prayers of thanksgiving, supplication or petition, and intercession all play a vital role in our combat against Satan, as do public and private praying. The Apostle especially calls for supplication as the key form of praying. We cannot succeed in our warfare apart from prayer that beseeches God to supply the strength and resolve we so profoundly need.

Then all this praying must be done "always." We are to "pray without ceasing" (1 Thess. 5:17). This doesn't mean that we're to do nothing but pray. That's impossible because Scripture clearly assigns us other responsibilities. But whatever we do is to be done with an attitude of prayer and a readiness to resort to prayer.

All of this is to be done "in the Spirit." We are to recognize our weakness apart from God, and we are to depend on the Spirit to give us the spirit of prayer, to help us formulate our petitions, and to give us the warmth of spirit and the fervency that prayer requires.

How the teaching of the apostle challenges and rebukes us! Most Christians have much to lament here. Our praying is often spasmodic, half-hearted, and haphazard. We're engaged in a most fearful warfare with a dreadful adversary, but we're also assured that our God occupies a throne of grace and that we can, through prayer, come there and "obtain mercy and find grace to help in time of need" (Heb. 4:16).

From time to time we hear accounts of individuals living as paupers while they have a fortune laid aside. We shake our heads in wonderment at such accounts. But many Christians are doing something very similar in the spiritual realm as they fail to draw help from the throne of grace through the privilege of prayer.

The church has always made her greatest advances when she most vigorously gave herself to prayer. Satan is not impressed with our personalities and our programs. But when the church prays, the earth trembles beneath her and Satan flees.

How blessed we are to have the Word of God and prayer! How foolish we are to not make better use of them!

-27-

From God's Word, the Bible...

...in everything give thanks; for this is the will of God in Christ Jesus for you.

1 Thessalonians 5:18

Living a "Ful"er Life (1)

The older I get, the more I realize how quickly this life is passing. I realize that it will soon be over, and I will be out in eternity. This makes me think about how I want to spend the rest of my days. First, I want to be *more thankful*. Every Christian can easily make a list of things he or she is thankful for—family, health, the beauties of creation, material possessions, as well as many other things. While we give thanks to the Lord for such things, we should be striving to be more conscious of them and more abundant in our praise.

There is, of course, one blessing that surpasses all others. The Apostle Paul says: "Thanks be to God for His indescribable gift" (2 Cor. 9:15).

Of all the gifts that God so generously gives, only one can be called "indescribable." That is the gift of His Son. That best-loved of all Bible verses, John 3:16, says: "For God so loved the world that He gave His only begotten Son that whoever believes in Him should not perish but have everlasting life."

Christians are very familiar with those words, and most would quickly agree that Christ is the best of all God's gifts. But even Christians can fail to realize just how grand that gift is. We know Jesus came to this earth as a man and that He died on the cross, but we don't always realize the true meaning of His death. Some admit that they don't understand how Jesus dying on a cross could provide salvation for us. The problem is that they are thinking of His death in physical terms only. We must never do that. Lots of men died on lots of crosses in those days, but Jesus' death was special. He received in the space of the six hours that He was on the cross the eternal wrath that our sins deserve. Because He was God in human flesh, He could receive that amount of wrath in that length of time.

When we truly understand what Jesus went through on that cross, we find it much easier to be more thankful. I don't want a day to go by without reflecting deeply on that cross, and, as I reflect, I want to pray the words of Fanny J. Crosby:

> *Let me love Thee more and more,*
> *'Till this fleeting, fleeting life is o'er;*
> *'Till my soul is lost in love,*
> *In a brighter, brighter world above.*
> *May Thy tender love to me*
> *Bind me closer, closer, Lord, to Thee.*

I also want to be more thankful for great public worship. Nothing so feeds and nourishes the soul as God-honoring, Christ-centered, Spirit-anointed worship. Alas, it seems to be harder and harder to find.

Good worship requires good preaching. I would like to hear preaching that is so anointed by the Spirit of God that I am, in the words of Charles Wesley, "lost in wonder, love and praise."

Preaching has been in a state of decline for several years. This isn't exactly a new thing. Centuries ago, John Calvin offered this lament:

> At the present day there are many who are well-nigh sickened by the very name of preaching, because there are so many stupid, ignorant men who blurt out their worthless brainwaves from the pulpit.[4]

But there have also been eras of powerful preaching. Oh, to see such an era again!

Good worship also requires robust congregational singing. To me, loud, boisterous, triumphant, and happy congregational singing is one of the finest things on this side of heaven. Such singing can lift the spirits of sad saints, and it can convince unbelievers that Christianity is a wonderful thing.

Still further, good worship requires consciousness of being in the presence of the majestic, glorious and holy God. Oftentimes "worship services" seem to be more devoted to entertaining the hearers and cultivating an air of lightheartedness and frivolity than they are to standing in awe of God. My wife and I are thankful to be members of a church that truly seeks to honor the Lord.

As life continues to pass, I'm coaching myself to making it "ful"-er, and the first of my "fuls" is thankful—thankful for all of God's blessings, but especially for the salvation provided by Christ and for worship that truly honors Him.

---

[4] Cited by Tom Lyon, "The Centrality of Preaching," Banner of Truth Magazine, November, 2005, p. 10

-28-

From God's Word, the Bible...

Finally then, brethren, we urge and exhort in the Lord Jesus that you should abound more and more, just as you received from us how you ought to walk and to please God. . . .

1 Thessalonians 4:1

Living a "Ful"er Life (2)

I want in the days that I have remaining to be more thankful. I also want to be *more prayerful*. Prayer is amazing to me. I can speak here on earth and be heard in heaven by the God who made all things and rules over all things to His eternal glory.

When I pray, I'm heard in heaven by the gracious God who planned my salvation, and by the Lord Jesus who purchased it for me on the cross. Heard in heaven! What a privilege! And what a God! Out of all the prayers that ascend to Him, He hears mine as if it were the only one being offered.

The amazing nature of prayer invariably makes me think of another amazing thing, namely, that I don't pray more than I do! To have the ear of God and not avail myself of it! What utter folly!

I've prayed all through my years, but never as much and never as well as I should have. In my older years, I want to do better. I want to be often at my Father's throne, offering adoration and praise, confessing my sins, thanking Him for His blessings, and seeking His grace. I want especially to besiege heaven with the prayer that God will do a mighty work in these days, elevating the gospel, reviving His church, and sweeping souls into His kingdom.

As I pray, I always want to remember that what I'm doing is a blood-bought privilege. I wouldn't have access to God at all if it weren't for the fact that Jesus shed His blood on the cross to purchase that access for me.

At this stage of life, I also want to be *more heedful*. I'm talking about paying closer attention to the commandments of the Lord. I want to be more holy. No matter how much holiness a Christian might attain in this life, there's always more to attain. Paul was undoubtedly a holy man, but he confessed that he needed to go further, saying: "Brethren, I do not count myself to have apprehended; but. . . I press toward the goal. . ." (Phil. 3.13a, 14a).

We sorely need to return to stressing holiness in living. Christians are often told these days that someone who says we should keep the Ten Commandments is being legalistic. But it's not legalism to keep what God has commanded. Legalism is requiring God's people to keep something that God hasn't commanded.

The lack of emphasis on holiness in our churches has led to Christians being more and more like the world and it has lessened our influence on the world. Our modern society is having much more success influencing us than we are influencing it.

As I set myself to be more holy in the future, I realize that I've never regretted those times in which I've kept the Lord's commandments. I've always regretted those times in which I didn't.

Finally, I want to be *more hopeful*. There is no uncertainty in the Christian's hope. It isn't a matter of the Christian being unsure about the future and crossing his fingers while he longs for the best. Hope is confident and joyful expectation. It is the Christian knowing what the future holds for him, and rising on his tiptoes with eager expectation to see it. It's the Christian looking forward to meeting Jesus in the air (1 Thess. 4:17) and to inhabiting a new earth in a new body.

Christians are always at their very best when they are most heavenly minded. I want to be more heavenly minded the nearer I get to heaven.

Now you have my "ful"s. There could be more, but I certainly don't want there to be less than thankful, prayerful, heedful, and hopeful. Many of these are expressed in this hymn by Philip Bliss:

> *More holiness give me, more striving within;*
> *More patience in suff'ring; more sorrow for sin;*
> *More faith in my Savior, more sense of His care;*
> *More joy in His service, more purpose in prayer.*

> *More gratitude give me, more trust in the Lord;*
> *More pride in His glory, more hope in His word;*
> *More tears for His sorrows, more pain at His grief;*
> *More meekness in trial, more praise for relief.*

> *More purity give me, more strength to o'ercome;*
> *More freedom from earth-stains, more longings for home;*
> *More fit for the kingdom, more used would I be;*
> *More blessed and holy, more, Savior, like Thee.*

-29-

From God's Word, the Bible...

Inasmuch as many have taken in hand to set in order a narrative of those things which have been fulfilled among us, just as those who from the beginning were eyewitnesses and ministers of the word delivered them to us, it seemed good to me also, having had perfect understanding of all things from the very first, to write to you an orderly account, most excellent Theophilus, that you may know the certainty of those things in which you were instructed.

Luke 1:1-4

Are You a Theophilus?

Luke, whom Paul calls "the beloved physician" (Col. 4:14), wrote two of the books of the New Testament. One is the Gospel that bears his name. The other is the book of Acts. Each of these books was addressed to a man named Theophilus (Luke 1:3; Acts 1:1).

Some think that Luke didn't have a specific individual in mind when he wrote his books. They suggest that he simply used the name Theophilus for any and all of his readers who loved God. But two details that Luke mentions about Theophilus suggest that he, Luke, actually addressed his books to a man by that name.

One of those details is Luke's use of the phrase "most excellent" to describe Theophilus (Luke 1:3). That indicates that Theophilus was a cultured man of high social standing. That makes it very unlikely that Luke was using the name Theophilus as a generic name for all of his readers, as many of them wouldn't have fallen into the category of highly cultured.

Another detail about Theophilus is that he had been instructed in the Christian faith (v. 3) but was evidently experiencing some uncertainty about it. This also indicates that he was a real person. Many of Luke's readers would not have been experiencing the uncertainty that Theophilus was feeling.

But while I assume that Theophilus was an actual individual, he does, in fact, represent those who lack certainty about Christianity. I recently read an article which indicated that most of those who have turned away from the Christian faith say it's because they no longer believe it to be true. The article gave these reasons from three young people who abandoned Christianity:

- "Learning about evolution when I went away to college";
- "Rational thought makes religion go out the window";
- "I just realized somewhere along the line that I didn't really believe it."

It's especially interesting that one student cited evolution as his reason for rejecting Christianity in light of the fact that the more we learn about DNA, the less tenable evolution seems.

And what shall we say to the student who thinks that "rational thought" makes Christianity impossible? We might ask if he or she considers it to be a rational thing to believe something for which there is abundant evidence.

Some people have the notion that there is no evidence for Christianity at all, and that believing it requires laying aside reason to make a blind leap into the dark without any basis for doing so.

There are lots of Theophiluses around. They have had some instruction in Christianity, but they are uncertain about it. Some, like the students mentioned above, have completely abandoned the Christian faith. Others still hold to it, but they do so without any depth of conviction. Like Theophilus of old, they lack certainty about the very thing that they profess to believe.

We don't know how Theophilus came to get in contact with Luke, but it was good for him that he did. Luke was able to assure him that there is "certainty" (v. 4) about "those things which are most surely believed among us" (v. 1).

Luke was talking about the Lord Jesus Christ, as his Gospel and the book of Acts go on to make clear. Christianity is Christ. Take Christ away, and there is no Christianity. Why should we believe in the Lord Jesus Christ? We have substantial evidence for Him. Luke mentions "eyewitnesses" (v. 2). He also claims that he himself had "perfect understanding" of those things that the eyewitnesses reported. With that phrase "perfect understanding," Luke is telling us that he had thoroughly researched the things that were asserted about Christ and had come to the conclusion that they were valid and true. As a result of his research, he was now ready to write his own account of the life and ministry of Jesus.

The Bible plainly declares that there's no need for us to be uncertain about Jesus. It urges us to take a long, hard look at the evidence, and bow before Him as our Savior and Lord. It's always sad when someone chooses to be an unbeliever, but the saddest of all unbelievers is the one who refuses to even look at the evidence for Christ. More about that in the next reading!

-30-

From God's Word, the Bible...

The former account I made, O Theophilus, of all that Jesus began both to do and teach, until the day in which He was taken up, after He through the Holy Spirit had given commandments to the apostles whom He had chosen, to whom He also presented Himself alive after His suffering by many infallible proofs, being seen by them during forty days and speaking of the things pertaining to the kingdom of God.

Acts 1:1-3

What Is the Evidence for Jesus?

What does the Bible affirm about Jesus? It maintains that He was the God-man, that is, God in human flesh and that He came to this earth in order to provide salvation for sinners. Jesus Himself put it in these words: "...the Son of Man has come to seek and to save that which was lost" (Luke 19:10).

Are these claims true? Was Jesus really the God-man? Did He actually provide salvation for sinners? In our previous reading we met Theophilus, who was uncertain about these things even though he had received instruction concerning them.

In the opening verses of his Gospel, Luke addressed Theophilus and assured him that he could be certain about the Lord Jesus. The Christian faith is not a leap in the dark. It's not a matter of the Christian crossing his fingers and hoping his beliefs prove to be true.

In his Gospel, Luke laid out things that Jesus said and did

(v. 1). His words alone constitute substantial evidence that He was, in fact, God in human flesh. In Luke 4:22, we read: "So all bore witness to Him and marveled at the gracious words which proceeded out of His mouth."

Then there were Jesus' deeds. Luke tells us that Jesus healed the sick (4.38-40; 5:12-15,17-26; 6:6-11,17-19; 7:1-10; 8:43-48, etc.), cast out demons (4:41; 8:26-39), raised the dead (7:11-17; 8:49-56), stilled a storm (8:22-25), and fed a multitude (9:10-17).

In addition to these things, three of His disciples saw Him in His heavenly glory on the Mount of Transfiguration (9:28-36).

Luke closes his Gospel by affirming that Jesus Himself arose from the grave (24:1-43) and ascended to the Father in heaven (24:50-53).

We should keep in mind as we read Luke's accounts of the miracles of Jesus that they were performed before the "eyewitnesses" that he mentions in the opening words of his Gospel (Luke 1:2).

When Luke took up his pen to write the book of Acts, it was so he could continue the story of Jesus. Some people seem to have the idea that Acts is all about the Holy Spirit, but, no, it is about the Lord Jesus. The Holy Spirit was the gift of Christ to His church, and the Holy Spirit's mission in this world is to exalt and glorify Christ.

Luke begins the book of Acts in the same way that he ended his gospel, that is, with the resurrection and ascension of Jesus.

Luke, along with all the early Christians, regarded the resurrection of Jesus as the supreme proof of His claims. No one can read the book of Acts without being impressed with how much emphasis the early disciples gave to the resurrection of Jesus. Luke tells us that Jesus "presented Himself alive after His suffering by many infallible proofs" (v. 3).

Many infallible proofs! Not one or two, but many! And not fabricated things, but proofs! And proofs that are not questionable or debatable but are infallible, that is, unmistakable or unassailable.

In his Gospel, Luke gives some of these many infallible proofs: the large stone covering the tomb of Jesus was rolled away, the body of Jesus was not in the tomb, angels were present to proclaim the resurrection, the cloths in which the body of Jesus had been wrapped were convincingly arranged, and the risen Christ appeared to many (Luke 24:1-43).

The appearances of the risen Christ had to be especially convincing in light of the fact that they were not limited to a single day or two, but were rather stretched out for a period of forty days.

Still another proof of Jesus' resurrection is the tremendous change that His disciples experienced. They went from being resurrection skeptics to being bold advocates of it. And, as the book of Acts so wonderfully details, the truth of Jesus' resurrection took Christianity from a tiny beginning to worldwide influence

We can also add to Jesus' resurrection the truth of His ascension (vv. 9-11), which was also witnessed by many.

The words, deeds, resurrection of Jesus, and ascension of Jesus come together to give us the overwhelmingly powerful testimony that He was indeed God in human flesh, the Savior for sinners, and that He lives today in the glory of heaven.

The question has never been whether there is sufficient evidence for Christianity. It has always been whether we will accept the evidence.

What about you? Are you challenged and encouraged by the words Luke wrote to Theophilus? Are you persuaded, not just intellectually, but in a way that has brought you to warm, personal faith in the Christ who came to bring a full and free salvation to all who turn from sin and trust in Him alone?

-31-

From God's Word, the Bible...

"Father, I desire that they also whom You gave Me may be with Me where I am, that they may behold My glory which You have given Me; for You loved Me before the foundation of the world."

John 17:24

"'Till We Meet Again"

A Reading from Sylvia

I was recently blessed to be part of a special reunion. For the last three years my four brothers and I, along with spouses, have been gathering once a year to spend two or three days together. We live in three different states, so time spent with all five of us together rarely happens. Since we are in our 60s and 70s, we realize that we need to be intentional about getting together. Life is speeding by, and we know the time will come when, one by one, we will be departing this life.

This year our sibling reunion was a little different. We invited another group of three siblings, whom we have known since childhood, to join us. These two brothers and a sister attended the same small country church as our family, and our parents were best friends. Growing up, we spent a lot of time together. It was so good to reminisce about our escapades as children and teenagers. One great blessing was sharing memories of our godly parents and the great impact they had on our lives.

It was mentioned more than once during the weekend that

we may never all be together again. I was reminded of a scene from my childhood related to that small country church we all attended.

Our church had experienced an unusual revival meeting, the kind today's younger generation of churchgoers know little or nothing about. I'm sure it was at least a two-week meeting, as all of them were in the 1950s. Some meetings even extended into the third week.

In this particular revival, we had experienced an unusual working of the Spirit of God in our midst. Unbelievers had become believers. Wayward believers had been revived. Church members who were at odds with one another had been reconciled. The presence of the Holy Spirit was evident in the worship services each night. As church members went about their day's work, their thoughts were on the joys of the previous evening's service and the anticipation of the coming evening's service. Even as a child, I experienced this blessed phenomenon.

The guest preacher for this revival meeting preached with an unusual anointing of God. In addition to this, he had a warm, winsome spirit about him. Our hearts were knit to him for the person he was, and for the work that God was doing through him.

On the last Sunday of the meeting, the church had planned a potluck farewell dinner for the guest preacher. After the morning preaching service, as we always called it, we went a short distance down the road to the two-room country schoolhouse for the dinner. We had the meal there because at that time our church had no fellowship hall or room large enough to have a meal together.

After the meal was over, the time came for our guest preacher to leave us and return to his home. He lived a long distance from our church, so we were keenly aware that we might never see him again in this life. And, oh, how we had come to love him! He had been God's instrument to bring great blessing to our church. Before he left, we formed a circle around the perimeter of that large room. We held hands and sang the words of Jeremiah Eames Rankin:

> *God be with you 'till we meet again;*
> *By His counsels guide, uphold you;*
> *With His sheep securely fold you.*
> *God be with you 'till we meet again.*
> *'Till we meet, 'till we meet,*
> *'Till we meet at Jesus' feet;*
> *'Till we meet, 'till we meet,*
> *God be with you till we meet again.*

Those of us who attended my family's special reunion may meet again in this life, but that is far from certain. I hope, if we never get together again on this earth, we will meet again at Jesus' feet in heaven's glory where our dear parents are already in the presence of the Lord. Nothing in this world is more important than making sure we are at the feet of Jesus in the eternal world. We can only be sure of that if we bow before Him in this life in true repentance and faith, taking what He did on the cross for sinners as our own. Let each of us heed these words from the Apostle Peter: "Therefore, brethren, be even more diligent to make your calling and election sure. . ." (2 Peter 1:10).

About the Authors

Roger Ellsworth is a retired pastor, active in ministry and writing, who lives in Jackson, Tennessee. He and his wife, Sylvia, love the message of the Bible, and they enjoy sharing the wonderful counsel of the Word of God in language that ordinary people can understand and appreciate.

In addition to being a wife and homemaker, Sylvia is a diligent student of Scripture and the busy grandmother of Daniel, Emmalee, Noah, Isaiah, and Eramin.

Roger has written numerous books on the Christian faith, and has exercised a preaching ministry for over fifty years. His sermons are available to listen for free on SermonAudio.com.

The Series

Enjoy collecting the My Coffee Cup Meditations Series.

A Dog and A Clock 978-0-9988812-9-4 (Series#1)
The "Thumbs-Up" Man 978-0-9988812-5-6 (Series#2)
When God Blocks Our Path 978-0-9988812-4-9 (Series#3)
Fading Lines, Unfading Hope 978-0-9996559-1-7 (Series#4)
The Day the Milk Spilled 978-0-9965168-6-0 (Series#5)
"Where Are the Donuts?" 978-0-9965168-7-7 (Series#6)
Sure Signs of Heavenly Hope 978-0-9988812-1-8 (Series#7)
My Dog Knows It's Sunday 978-0-9996559-6-2 (Series#8)
Rover and the Cows 978-0-9996559-7-9 (Series#9)
Apples of Gold in Silver Settings 978-0-9600203-0-0 (Series#10)
Old Houses, New Houses 978-0-9600203-1-7 (Series#11)
Golden Key and Silver Chain 978-0-9600203-2-4 (Series#12)

Get the set for a special price:

www.mycoffeecupmeditations.com/crazyoffer

Collect All the Books!

www.mycoffeecupmeditations.com

www.ingramcontent.com/pod-product-compliance
Lightning Source LLC
Chambersburg PA
CBHW050555300426
44112CB00013B/1931